# THE SACRED AWAKENING OF LIGHT WARRIORS

## *Channelled Lessons from the Counsel of Light*

**Victoria Jimenez**

*Cover art and illustrations by*
Seema Chandru Keswani

Circle Enterprises (London) Ltd.

This first edition published in 2002 by
Circle Enterprises (London) Ltd.
Siddeley House, 50 Canbury Park Rd.
Kingston-upon-Thames, Surrey KT2 6LX
England

Editors: Laura High, Cara Cantarella, Rebecca Young
Production: Sandra Goodrich

Printed in Great Britain on recycled paper
by GHL Solutions Ltd, London, E9 5EN

A catalogue record of this book is
available from the British Library

ISBN 0-9540915-0-7

To my mother, Sylvia Atiles-Lovelace I recognize who you are and thank you for showing me how to claim myself. Thank you for your example of love and light. Thank you for the many times that you have put me in front of the greatest spiritual masters of our present time, and at an early age. I am forever grateful and hope I live my life as beautifully as the beautiful example you are.

Finally, to all the masters and teachers on both sides of the veil, thank you for your tireless efforts at helping the planet awaken. It gives me an example of faith, love and light.

The Beginning Without End made sure I had absolutely everything I needed to complete this project. God bless you all. Peace be your journey.

# Table of Contents

*Lovingly dedicated to both Barbara Ann Brennan,*
*teacher, healer, channel, and scientist extraordinaire.*
*You saved my life. Thank you.*
*And*
*To Sylvia Lovelace.*
*You gave me life*
*and guided me.*
*Thank you.*

# Acknowledgements

This book is the result of the love and the work of many people that I wish to thank. It is only with their undying commitment that this work is complete. For each of you who has contributed, I offer my love, gratitude and thanks.

To Marilyn, Michael, and Miranda, thank you for the lessons on love. To Marilyn, thank you for choosing to stay in order for me to have my purpose. The guides are right. I would not have been able to do this if you had crossed over. Not a moment goes by where I am not thanking the Creator for the gift of you. I will never forget you.

To everyone at Circle Enterprises (London) Ltd., and Unitive Consciousness International, you are my family. Sandy, thank you for your expertise and love – you truly are the Presence, a blessing from God, a treasured friend.

To my editors Cara Cantarella, Laura High, and Rebecca Young, I thank God for you every day. You are nothing short of brilliant. Excellence at its peak. You are the healers of the written word. To Becky, there are no words capable of expressing my gratitude at just having your presence in my life. You are a wonderful business partner, healer, teacher, and friend. It proves there is a God. To Laura, friend, editor, counselor, and patient, loving, amazing soul. This would never have gotten off the ground without your dedication, love, support, professional skill, patience, and vision. I am eternally grateful to the Creator for the gift of you. You are the miracle worker. Thank you for believing in me when I did not. Thank you to Joel, for all his computer skills, humor and boundless love, boundless enthusiasm, boundless playfulness and boundless light.

Thank you to Seema. There are angels on the planet. You are one of them, an angel on the planet, sent by the Creator to spread unconditional love. Thank you for putting so much love into the art in and on the book. May the world receive your healing gift of love. Thank you to Cindy for helping me to stand in my truth and integrity. Thank you for helping me find pieces of my lost self and catalyzing me into self-responsibility.

To my sister Edie, thank you for your wonderful sense of humor and your magic of making something happen out of nothing. You have been a teacher to me and have not even known. To my sister Laurie, every person has a hero, someone they look up to and admire. There may be a quality about them that you love and appreciate. Your gift to me was and still is tenacity. You have been quietly, unknowingly, guiding me through my healing journey. You have grace, tenacity, and crazy wisdom. Namaste, dear sweet and wonderful soul, you are my hero. To the man I call my father, Lloyd, thank you for showing me how to live life on my own terms, to experience adventure no matter what the outcome, and to know that is truly the experience of living. To Nina, thank you for guiding my healing process. You are amazing and I will never forget you. You are wise, loving and sacred in my heart.

To Barbara Brennan, and the Barbara Brennan School of Healing, thank you for the container of healing that you hold for the Earth and her people, that also includes me, and to the teaching staff at BBSH, GOD BLESS YOU ALL. It is a blessing in my life to have attended the most extraordinary school in history.

# Preface

I wish that I could tell my dear reader that I had an extensive background and some great degree regarding this subject. Or maybe that I had been a professor for several years at a prestigious university. Or that I had spent several years studying with a shaman elder from some far-away tribe in an exotic land. That way this material might hold a little more weight with the reader. Isn't that why we consult books written by experts?

I wish that I could declare more expertise so that when you, the reader, read these lessons, you will feel with your heart and know that they come from a group of experts on the other side of "the veil." I wish that I had more to declare, so that you won't miss your truth in these lessons sent by the Counsel of Light. I believe that many beings are on the planet now trying to help us awaken into a world of peace and love. However, none of them have degrees, and we certainly don't have an external gauge to determine which channeled readings will be the most beneficial to us. What we use is our heart. We feel the truth. We can ask our own Counsel to come together with us to help us find our truth. All we need to say is, "Show me the truth." May you find your truth in these lessons.

I do not know why the Counsel of Light chose to communicate these lessons through me. To be honest, I am not really concerned about why. What I care about is that their choice has helped my life become closer to the Creator. I would like to share my background with you. My degree is in Accounting, a subject I don't really like. So upon graduation, I did not know what to do with my life. I did not want to be an accountant. So I hemmed and hawed at little jobs until I decided to become a police officer. I did not dabble in spirituality. I thought that channeling was a con game and a bunch of bull. I did not believe in crystals or healing. In fact, I thought that people who believed in those things were weird. I thought they were hippie throwaways who couldn't get a life. I was a cynic, and I loved the prestige and power of being a police officer. It gave me a false sense of who I was that I could respect. I did not have a lot of self-love, and I could hide that behind my badge. My favorite place to be was on duty, in uniform. People instantly respected me. My life was heaven at that time. I had a great relationship and a great life. It was the first time in my 30-year life that I was happy.

My world would soon turn into my awakening. At that time, I lived in a house where the master bedroom was located in the basement. The room was dark and cool, which made it a pleasant place to sleep during the summer months. One night, it was approximately 2.30 a.m. and I was sound asleep. I do not know what prompted me to open my eyes. I was not having a bad dream. My eyes just popped open as if I had had enough sleep. Upon looking at the ceiling, I saw a big luminous thing. It lit up the room. However, instead of seeing it as an angel or something heavenly, I became so frightened that I pulled all the covers very quickly over my head. I felt like a young child again - as if there were monsters on my ceiling instead of under the bed.

My heart was pounding and I felt a lot of panic. I reached over to my spouse, who was by now awake enough to ask me what was the matter. I replied, "Look at the ceiling, look at the ceiling - what is that?"

"What's what? I don't see anything."

I popped my head out of the covers to see only dark. I shook the fear off and rationalized that maybe I had had a bad dream, and that I hadn't really seen anything. As I rocked myself back to sleep, I would again experience another awakening . . . this time in my dream state.

I do not remember the whole dream. I only remember a small part, which happens to be the most significant part. I am walking down a dirt road with a couple of other women. We are pulling a cart filled with dried fruit. We are meeting another group of women who have vegetables in a cart. We are going to trade some dried fruit for some vegetables. Somehow I have the feeling that we live in communities that are similar to communes. As we meet the other group of women, introductions are being made. I can't remember names. I only remember someone saying, "This woman here channels Jesus Christ." I stop with total cynicism and say, "Well, that is pretty big." I don't quite know what to say in my disbelief.

The woman turns to me and says, in a voice unlike any I've ever heard, "So you wish to see light?" She waves her hand over my head, as she says, "Now you see light." As I turn to look at everyone in the dream, an outline of brilliant blue is all around them. I waver between being totally fascinated by this and yet afraid. I wonder if it will go away, or if it has an on-off switch. It is such brilliant blue.

I then awaken from the dream. I get up and start up the stairs to the bathroom. I pass the kids and they have brilliant blue around them. I pass the dog and I see blue. Now again I become frightened. I go to the bathroom and rub my eyes and laugh to myself, "Oh, Vickie, you're seeing things left over from a dream. It'll go away."

It didn't go away, though. Days went by, and I was still seeing things around people, animals, and trees. I was becoming tired and sick to my stomach. I was afraid to sleep, because I thought that there was something wrong with me, and that whatever it was, it happened in my sleep. I went to doctors, all kinds of doctors- eye, gland, family practice, and gynecologist. Even when they had poked, thumped, probed, and pictured all of me, they could not find anything wrong with me. They determined that my next course of action was to call a shrink and take some anti-depressants, because I could very well have post-traumatic stress disorder from being a police officer.

I was very depressed, and I was afraid that I would never get out of the depression. I was scared that I would become suicidal. The depression began to interfere with my relationship and my ability to perform my job. My wonderful loving partner and spouse thought that I was becoming schizophrenic. We did not know what to do. So, off I went to see a psychologist. This, too, gave me a lot of fear. I was certain that I was going to be put somewhere for observation. I did not know if I would ever get out. By now my relationship was in shambles and it would never again regain its luster. This truly broke my heart. It was the worst pain I have ever been through.

While I was at the psychologist's office, the psychologist asked me what I was seeing. I described it for her, explaining everything. I also told her that I would not take anti-depressants or any other form of medication because I wanted to find the cause of my illness, not mask its symptoms. She agreed and we proceeded. She had me draw what I saw and describe it. I would give her details about the beings which were floating around. One day, while I was speaking to her about what I was seeing, the psychologist asked, "What are they saying?" This made me very angry. I thought she was trying to find out just how crazy I was. So I yelled at her, saying, "I can't hear them – I can only see them!!!!"

She said, "All right, all right," and pulled a big blue book from her bookshelf. Showing me the pictures in the book, she asked if this was what I was seeing. Lo and behold, it *was* what I was seeing – in greater detail than I could see. The book was *Hands of Light*, written by Barbara Ann Brennan. I felt a big sense of relief at having discovered that I might not be crazy. I went home after that wonderful session with my therapist and slept.

A couple of days later, my sister and my family were out finally relaxing together. I felt relieved and happy for the first time in several months. My sister's family and my family were on a picnic together, and we were also doing some "lookie-lu" shopping. We went into a book store and there was that big blue book laying on the table – several copies of it. But the price was out of my range. I didn't care, though. Just looking at that book made me feel good. I felt safe for the first time in a long time.

I must have had a twinkle of fascination looking at that book. We left the bookstore and got in the car. I was planning to buy a copy of the book when I had a little more money. As my family drove off, I sat in the back just feeling good. Then my sister flopped the big blue book in my lap and said, with a cheerful "gotcha" look, "I saw ya eye-ballin' it – besides, maybe you can learn to do this, too." A few days later, while I was looking at one of the beings, I suddenly could hear them speak to me: "My name is One Who Is Wise." And thus, the dance of awakening began.

After two years of therapy and studying and listening to the guides, I made the decision to enroll in the Barbara Brennan School of Healing in New York, (now based in Miami, Florida) which I have now graduated from. The Counsel of Light showed themselves to me about three months before I was to start school. They asked me to write down these lessons on paper. And so I have. May they bring you love and light.

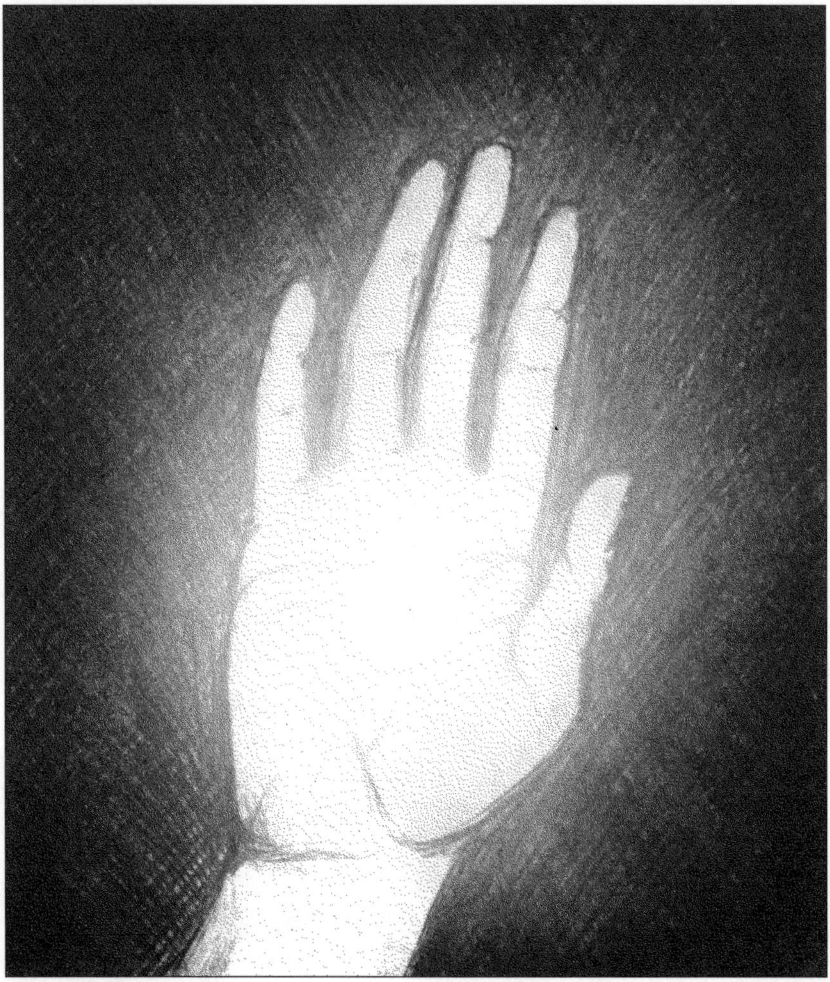

# Introduction

Hello, my name is Victoria Jimenez, and I have never written an introduction before. In fact, I have never written anything more than a high school homework report on some subject or country. This is certainly a brand new experience for me. I am still frightened about what people will think, say, and do because of the writings I am about to present.

I do not have a degree in psychology or years of study in a subject related to what I have been asked to write. I am a very average person who has a very average life. I do, however, have faith, love, courage, and a great support system (on both sides of the veil) that have helped me put together the channelled teachings in this book. It is more than an honor that I was chosen to help impart the Counsel's message in the form of words.

Please go within and feel the truth. It is the way of this dimension of the physical world to only believe that which we can taste, touch, smell, hear, feel, and see. Often, while an individual is busy paying bills and going to work in a downtown office, he or she can forget that there are other senses that go beyond the reality you may take for granted. A person can certainly become lost, if you will, almost as if he or she were a sheep or a cow being led to who-knows-where.

We have lost a lot of our self-awareness and soul's expression. The intention of the Counsel of Light is to reintroduce ourselves to our whole selves – the parts that we have buried, ignored, or forgotten. The Counsel's intention is to help each of us remember who we really are and not who we have believed ourselves to be based on the illusions of other people's beliefs, or the indulgence of fear and control.

I want to talk about genetics here. If you are musical or mathematical, then there is a good chance that one of your children will be musical or mathematical, or both. Similar "genetics" apply for the children of the Creator. We are made with the same energies of creation and we are creators. Creation is within us. We create our own lives. I feel that if I know this, and I can own this piece of myself, then I can now be responsible for creating my life with intention and unity. I can realize that I have all the help and abundance that I wish to have.

I feel that the Counsel of Light wishes to give the physical dimension the truth about wholeness – the Gestalt view of the dimensions. They wish to help you to know yourself as a multi-dimensional being; to find the piece of creation that you are; and to find the true essence of your self. They wish to help you bring light to the parts of yourself that are still caught within the poisons of the soul and to bring love energy to the self.

The Counsel of Light is a group of beings who inhabit a different dimension, also called "the other side of the veil." Each member of the Counsel is an energy representation of the Creator. The Counsel wishes to help the Creator at this time in history, when there are so many people on the planet who are here to help themselves awaken and evolve into the age of peace and unity.

The twelve energies that make up the Counsel are: the Voice, Knowing, Truth, Wisdom, Sound, Tone, Presence, Teacher, Male (or Yang), Female (or Yin), Color, and of course, Love. These energies exist just as the Creator does – they are in everything. They are what the Earth is created from.

They are also what you are created from. They can be considered life-force energies.

If we look at the members of the Counsel as energies, just as we look at electricity, then we can study them in physical form. If we study the energy of Wisdom, for instance, we can explore just how it works. Wisdom energy is a gift from the Creator. It is not something we create or own. Wisdom existed before you did. Before you were born, Wisdom was helping create. Wisdom energy helped you with the task of your incarnation. Wisdom energy helped create the Earth and the heavens. Wisdom helped create you.

It is helpful to start seeing Wisdom as the ever-present energy it is, rather then something you earn or have. If we see that the energy of Wisdom is what we were created with, and that it is in and of itself whole, we can then begin to communicate with it. We can learn how to utilize Wisdom in our everyday lives, to help us with our personal healing. We can find out how to use the Counsel of Wisdom. This can be said for all twelve of the Counsel members. It is the same for Truth, Presence, and all of the others.

Truth is another energy that has been here since before you were created. Truth is an energy that you were created from. In order for you to integrate Truth, you must first see that it is a gift from the Creator. This understanding of Truth follows the same principle as does the understanding of Wisdom. You may apply this understanding to all twelve energies. Each energy has its gift, its special unique purpose to convey.

Now for the chemistry lesson of this section. Just as other energies combined create something, so does the combination of energies which make up the Counsel of Light. We understand that if we combine two hydrogen atoms with one oxygen atom, we create water. Water is made up of two unique types of atom, but these two things together create a totally new substance. Hydrogen is whole in and of itself. Oxygen is whole in and of itself. So is water. That new substance has wholeness. Standing alone, it is the wholeness of water. Water has many gifts. It can be ice, ocean, snow, steam, rain, hail, river, lake, or morning dew. Whichever form water wants to take, it can take. In order to create a molecule of water, we must have the required combination of atoms.

This is the extent of my chemistry ability. What, then, is created when we combine all twelve energies of the Counsel of Light? We create a light being - a magnificent being of all twelve energies, glistening full of the Creator's love. That's what we are. We have forgotten who and what we are. Also, we exist in different combinations and colors, and with different gifts. Some have the gift of healing; others have the gifts of art, music, dance, or math and science. All of these gifts spring from particular combinations of the twelve energies that comprise us. This chemistry analogy represents the way in which we are created in the image of the Father.

The Counsel is made up of the single form of each of the individual energies used in creation. It would be as if hydrogen and oxygen each came to speak to us individually and give us the Counsel of water. Hydrogen might tell us what his part was; oxygen would explain his part, too. Thus, the term for twelve single energies coming to speak to the great beings of light is "the Counsel of Light."

Why have these energies come to give us their counsel? They have come because it is the time on Earth of the Great Awakening. It is a time of healing, clearing, and transformation . . . which brings us to the lessons in this book. Before we transform our awareness of who we are, we must know what we truly are. Transformation automatically starts to happen when we discover the truth of who we are. These are lessons in awakening who we truly are. It is my prayer that they provide you, the reader, with the greatest good, towards your best and highest interest. For myself, it is my prayer that these lessons bring me into a closer and deeper relationship with the Great Spirit. I look forward to my next lesson. Thank you, Counsel of Light, for blessing my life with the grace of God. There truly is no greater gift.

## Lesson One:
# The World Beyond Separation

Welcome, dear ones.

We are the Voice, the Knowing and the Truth. We use these names to help you while in your physical and dualistic world. We call ourselves the Counsel of Light. It is our joy to bring you truth, wisdom, and love. We do not need to explain that we are helpers. It is a task of love and joy for us to be here at such an incredible period in the whole existence of what you call "time."

There have never been as many people on the planet as there are right now, at this point in what you call "history." There has never been so much violence on the planet as there is right now. There has never been so much upheaval in governments as there is right now. There has never been so much pollution on the planet as there is right now. There have never been so many different religions on the planet as there are right now. There have never been so many healers on the planet as there are right now.

You may ask yourself, dear one, "Why did I choose to be here during this period in time? I could have picked another time in history to be born, and why did I choose to be here now? What is the purpose of my birth at this time in history?"

We, the Counsel of Light, wish to tell you that it is no accident that you are here. You were asked by the Creator, God, Buddha, or whatever name you may use, to be here. You were asked and chose to be here for your growth and to help awaken the world. You have known all your life that there was something big and important for you to do. We are here to help you awaken to your task and remember who you are. You are the bringers of the age of newness. We are the Counsel of Light. We are here to serve, love, educate, and – most importantly – open you to what is truly available to you.

It is no accident that you found this book. It is no accident that you are on the planet at this time. You can feel in your heart that it is no accident. There is something that you are to do to help yourself, the world, and its awakening. This journey will bring you joy, abundance, and happiness. Peace be your journey, dear ones. It is a gift of love that we meet.

* * * * *

*The light that shines from within is the passion.*
*It is my food, my clothing.*
*It is my anchor.*
*It is my destiny.*
*It is the way of the path.*

* * * * *

I am the Voice.

I welcome you to the lesson. Today we speak of love and light, the world beyond separation. As you exist on the planet, we exist on what you call "the other side of the veil." When you are born into the physical, you slowly forget where you came from, why you are here, and that you are a being of light. You become trapped in the physical world and believe it is the only world that exists. You pray, meditate, talk to angels, or read books on people that have talked to angels. All the while you have forgotten that you started on "our side" of the veil first. You might believe that there are two sides of the veil. What you might not believe is that both sides of the veil exist at one time, in one place.

Your ancestors lived on both sides of the veil. The native people of many countries communicated with both sides of the veil all the time, every day. (Some still do.) You have just forgotten how to do this. The mountains speak, the trees speak. All things speak with their own voice. They also live on both sides of the veil at the same time. Many of your favorite teachers and medicine men and women talk to animals, plants, trees, guides, angels, and Creator. They understand that they are part of a world that already exists. They also know that they are as much a part of that world as they are the physical world. They understand that there is no difference between the two worlds. They understand that it is not some magic happening in their lives.

You may say, "That is what makes those native teachers great and special." This is true. However, this understanding is also available to you any time you want to receive it. You may say that you have tried to relate to the other side of the veil, and when you talk to them you do not hear them. It is our hope that reading the words of the Counsel of Light will help you manifest the actions that are most related to your purpose, know how to eliminate the imaginary veil, and come bathe in the love and wisdom of the Creator.

The worlds that exist have been called "heaven and earth." Both exist in the now. Time is a term used in the physical world. We discuss time because it is one of the traps that keeps you from contacting the other side of the veil. For example, in many countries Sunday is a holy day. Many people gather together on Sunday to worship and be with the counsel of the Creator. They have fellowship with other members of a particular group. They pray, feast, and celebrate because it is the "time" of the week designated for worship. Sometimes in the middle of the week they gather together to pray and worship because they have made this set time to do so. These activities all are time-focused. The concept of time keeps many of you preoccupied. So preoccupied in fact, that you cannot find your passions, feel life bubble within you, or speak to the One who is going to show you how to find your abundance. Time keeps you herded as if you were sheep.

What if the Creator wishes to seek communion with you? What if on Sunday morning the Creator says, "Wait. Don't go to the community place today. Sit with me in the living room of your home and *we* shall talk."

How do you create conversation with guides, angels and the Creator? To communicate means that two beings are talking to each other. You might think that people who believe they can talk with angels, guides, or the Unseen Presence are a little "out of touch." But many people talk to their plants and animals.

Another thing that keeps many people from communicating with this side of the veil is money. Some people believe they are not worthy unless they have a lot of money. They have to work so hard to get money that they are too tired to communicate with guides or angels or God. People believe that the Creator will not take care of them and that they must toil for their living. The feeling of unworthiness is another reason many people do not communicate with the other side of the veil.

It does not matter at what time in history this began. It does not matter who is responsible for all of the upheaval manifesting on the planet at this time. Blaming will not heal the soul of the Earth nor the hole that is in your heart at this time.

Most important, dear one, is that piece of you that has sat down to read this, hoping it will have some clues about the secret burning in your heart, the secret burning in your soul – that secret burning you think no one knows about that will not go away. You might think, "Why would anyone want me to help in the awakening of the world? I am not important. I can't awaken myself. I don't know how." It does not matter what you say to ignore that fire within. *It never goes away*. It was put there by the Creator. It will always keep you searching for that "something." That is why you picked up this book.

It is time to manifest that "something." Just feel your heart. At this time many of you have been called to the planet to help heal and bring in the age of newness. We call you warriors, but you are not warriors of violence. You are warriors of wisdom, warriors of love, warriors of light. Within you, great warrior one, is the key to the awakening of your soul, the awakening of your planet. Within you are locked the secrets of peace and harmony. You have been born with the task of manifesting these on the planet.

When you were on "our side" of the veil and were asked to do this work, you were excited and thought, "How wonderful a task." It is time for you to awaken. Dissolve the illusion of the veil between worlds and bring in the age of peace, love and light that has been foretold in your books of ancients, foretold by prophets and medicine men of the ages. Let your heart pound right now with all its questions of, "Is this true? Can this be real?" It is the only real truth. Everything else is an illusion. Peace be your journey, dear one. It is no accident that we meet.

* * * * *

*When I was a child, I knew.*
*When I am a child, I know.*
*When I am a child, I am confident.*
*When I am a child, I feel the earth.*
*When I am a child, I am truth.*
*When I am a child, I can see and feel heaven.*

* * * * *

## Lesson Two:
# Your Healing Purpose

We are the Counsel of Light.

We are the Voice, the Knowing, and the Truth. We use these names because you do not have words that describe the voice of creation, the knowing of creation or the truth of creation. It is not necessary for you to completely know everything about us to communicate. However, the Counsel is available to us all.

Each of you has your own counsel that will help you accomplish the purpose you have agreed to accomplish in this lifetime. Your counsel is with you to help you with your lessons, your gifts, and your world tasks. You may access your counsel through prayer and meditation. Your counsel has your best interest at heart. Your counsel knows you have been sent here to incarnate because you were chosen and agreed to be one of the Warriors of Light helping to bring in the age of newness.

This is no small task. It requires much bravery, faith, love, and strength that come from living many lifetimes. Your work here is as important to the universe as it is to you. You can surely feel how special your job is by how many other beings you are helping – for example, the plants, other animals, and Mother Earth herself.

Each of us is chosen for our specific task because we are the best one for the job. If you were a supervisor in a factory that had many individual jobs, you would determine who would be the most qualified person for each task. It is no different with you. You were chosen in the same manner for your ability to accomplish your task. You may not know what your task is, and that is not necessary at this time. That will unfold as you get closer to Creator.

What then can the Counsel help you with? Your counsel can help you learn how to connect with the Creator in your heart. Your counsel can teach you how to obtain guidance so that when your purpose manifests itself, you have assistance. Your counsel can help you find your purpose. It can show you how to find other Warriors of the Light and build community and good, healthy relationships with them. Your counsel can give comfort when you are in need. It can warn you of impending disasters and guide you to your task during these times of turbulence.

Your counsel most wants to tell you how *honored and loved* you are. It is more than you can feel in your heart or know in your soul. When you complete your work and come back home, the adoration and love you so richly deserve can be felt by you and expressed by us. For now, carry in your heart the knowledge of our love for you. Try and connect with that state of grace that exists in your heart. That is your counsel honoring you and your work. We offer a toast in your honor.

* * * * *

*That without beginning and without end*
*unites us all in oneness.*
*All have been chosen to accomplish.*
*All have been asked to help.*
*By saying "yes," we have committed.*
*We have honor. We have grace.*
*We have fearlessness.*

* * * * *

Welcome, all who seek the truth! We are the Counsel of Light. The Counsel is honored by your presence. You are honored, loved and respected. You have such a great task. It is no accident that you are reading this. You have been chosen by the One who is Without Beginning and Without End. It is in the presence of the wise ones and teachers, who have walked this planet before you, that we impart this knowledge.

* * * * *

*May all who gather in wisdom*
*sit at the table of the elders,*
*eat of the one true knowledge,*
*partake of its victory,*
*feel its love and kindness,*
*and celebrate the warrior within.*

* * * * *

I am the Voice.

I am the voice that is within all of you. I am the piece of God that exists within each human. I am the divine spark of inspiration, the longing for connection that keeps you searching endlessly for your true self. I am the keeper of your hidden wisdom. Before you are given the key to unlock your gifts, you are given the longing to find them. The search is inherent to your nature. Every man or woman on the earth at this time has within them the gifts that relate to their tasks. You keep them in your energy field, in your body, and in your brain. Your yearning has kept you always searching for the great "something." You have been through many trials and tribulations in your life with few answers. Much pain has been felt by each warrior, and no two pains are alike.

Each warrior has a personal purpose to do before his world purpose. You can compare it to boot camp. You learn to be a soldier before you are sent into battle. You must learn tactical skills, physical skills and how to care for yourself and your fellow soldiers in times of need. You go through rigorous training before you are a soldier for your cause. You learn many things about your fellow soldiers and yourself. You learn what skills you have and those of your fellow soldiers.

Why is this so important? Because when there is a crisis, you all have to work together to survive. Therefore, it is of the utmost importance to know which warrior has the best skills for each task. As warriors, we learn appreciation for each other's abilities. We do not envy our fellow warriors' talents. Instead, we express our thankfulness and joy with dignity. This natural evolution is not hard because you develop self-respect and respect for your own abilities. Before we can access our gifts, we must learn to appreciate our talents and the talents of our fellow warriors.

"Where are my gifts hiding?" you ask. I will tell you, Soldier of the Light. They are already within you. Beneath your childhood wounds are your gifts. Each of you is born into a physical body. At birth you know what your gifts are, and as time goes by you forget, which is as it should be. The only thing left is your yearning, your longing that speaks to you at night when your mind is at the soul level. You may have felt that you were somehow "chosen" and didn't know what for. You could feel an ache in your heart, a connection to something greater than you could imagine, some deep sense of importance, yet you could never quite find what it was. You wondered if anyone else felt the way you did and you became afraid that you were the only one with these deep feelings of something grander. You may have felt shame or unworthiness at having those feelings, and you quickly disconnected from that sacred remembering.

You didn't seem to "fit in" anywhere. You desperately wanted to connect with something but could not find anything that seemed to fit. In school you did not belong to one group but to all groups, and yet you were a loner. You understood other people, but no one ever seemed to quite understand you. You couldn't relate to people your own age, but you were too young to associate with adults, so you spent much time alone. You may have experienced a lot of *déjà vu*, maybe to the point that you considered it a common occurrence and never stopped to question it. You had early spiritual fascinations such as Eastern philosophy, Christianity, or dream analysis. Yet with all these interests, you found school boring. How lonely and discouraged you felt. You thought there was something wrong with you. You may have become depressed or turned to drugs, alcohol, or sex - anything to try and connect.

"Why," you ask, "did I have to experience this awful pain? This horrible place surely is no place for a warrior. No merciful God would put me here and then tell me I chose this. *No, I didn't!*"

A lot of warriors were born into dysfunctional families because they are the healers of that dysfunction. You cannot remember that you accepted that task because time has erased your memory. However, you were chosen for that job. Behind that task are your gifts, dear ones. Behind the pain is your world gift. The wonderful being that you are is behind the pain of healing that dysfunction. You were chosen to heal it *because you are the best soldier for that job.* Maybe you have tolerance, patience, love, or intuition – things that no one else in your family has. They are yours to help heal your lineage and yourself.

Allow the Voice to give an example. Before the white man came to America, there was a peaceful group of people living close to Mother Earth and Great Spirit. They were the native peoples of the land. But all their land was stolen and many were slaughtered, raped, and dishonored. The Native Americans felt despair and depression. Many of their ways were lost forever. There is still much anger that Native Americans feel. There is much sorrow, fear, and depression at the loss of their ways. The white man took without asking and forced the Indian children to learn his ways so they were not "savage" anymore.

So here you are, Soldier of the Light, helping bring in the age of newness. Helping man awaken into oneness. You are born into a "white" family but have some Native American heritage. Are you a white man or a red man? Are you embarrassed by what the white man did or do you feel that he had good intentions but went about it incorrectly? In your soul do you feel the pounding drums of your forefathers and grandfathers? Are you embarrassed by the drumming because no one else feels it? Are you pulled to your native side because it is popular now? Do you feel a deep sadness but don't know what it is? Do you ever hear something that sounds like people calling your name for help?

Where are you living, red and white man? Are you in a city? Why? Are you on a reservation? Why? Do you feel that you belong or don't belong to a race? Why? Are you embarrassed to be a red man? Why? Are you embarrassed to be white? Why? Do you see all the dysfunction and turmoil there is just to be born into the race culture? Are you to join these two angry races into oneness and unity? Are you the healer of that?

You can see, as a Soldier of the Light, that in order to help awaken from this turmoil into unity, the first thing you have to learn and accept is the fact you are the chosen warrior and that you are the best one for that job. Surely you can see that this healing would be something important to the universe. In order for the world to awaken into a state of peace and love, you must first look at your personal belief systems created by your past and some of your ancestors. There are many such tasks whether your heritage is Jewish or German, African-American or white. There are other abuses to heal as well.

Dear Soldiers of the Light, know that your purpose comes with many rewards as well. There are many things that we shall speak of later that are earthly rewards. In every man or woman there is a leader, a teacher, a healer, a lover, or an intuit. There are many great soldiers who awakened the warrior within, such as Martin Luther King, Gandhi, Crazy Horse, Abraham Lincoln and Harriet Tubman. The list could go on forever. What is your task my dear soldier? What is your healing purpose? These men and women were not born privileged. Nor were they helped by the privileged. They were, in fact, born into great disadvantage. Their circumstances were horrible.

What gifts did they bring to the human race? They brought the breath of God with them, freedom, peace, and spirituality. They had no memory of their task either. They all had that same pain and longing you have. Maybe at night they felt they were going to be special, too. Do you think they felt pain, anger, hurt, or depression like you? Yes, my dear ones, you are in good company. Follow your longing inside so you can manifest your purpose. Please remember that the only things that helped these other great soldiers in their struggles were their connections to the Beginning Without End and their personal connections to their tasks. All of these leaders had different religious faiths, but they had only one light in common: the light of God, Allah, Great Spirit. If all these wonderful soldiers of light left you with one message, what would they say to you?

Let the Voice tell you what the great warriors of light from your earth might say to you:

* * * * *

*We hear your whispers of greatness locked inside you.*
*In order for you to heal the pain of the world,*
*you must experience the pain of the world.*
*Don't lose yourself in the pain.*
*Follow your longing and pray*
*to the One who is Without Beginning and Without End.*
*Have faith.*
*Know that whatever you need to heal the pain*
*has been given to you already.*
*It is inside you and you must find it.*
*Believe that you have been sent here to awaken the world,*
*because you have been,*
*and that will help you find your path.*
*Believe in yourself and your task.*
*We do.*

* * * * *

You see, my soldiers, many soldiers of the past and present have been through the same pain as you. They have greatness and so do you. The Beginning Without End did not send you here to live in suffering. You were sent here to help *heal, teach, love, and have abundance*. Live at your highest potential. The Counsel wishes to help you find your path and connect to your "God" inside. In order to do this, we will give you basic tools to help you become a Warrior of the Light.

It is with much humility that the Counsel bows at your heart level for the work you already have done. We cannot express the love and honor all of you give the universe by choosing to awaken the planet as you have. There is so much work to do. It is time for all Warriors of the Light to gather together and make one nation of themselves. This is crisis time. There is no time to waste. Soon upon this planet will come great tragedies. Many already have happened. We are in need of your gifts and your help. It is our intention to help you manifest those gifts. Peace be to you this day as you read this. It is no accident that we meet.

* * * * *

*Out of the mud blooms the lotus flower.*
*Out of the darkness comes the light.*
*Out of the anger comes the love of God.*
*Out of the pain blooms the warrior.*
*May the glory of realization*
*penetrate the longing of the soul*
*and elevate the universe.*

* * * * *

## Lesson Three:
# What is a Light Warrior?

---

We are the Counsel of Light.

You are honored in your work and your quest for the truth. We want to extend our deepest love and respect for the warriors who have incarnated to do the work of helping all souls enter the new era of peace and love. In order to do that, you have incarnated into the unawareness of life to help the universe awaken. We cannot show you enough honor or tell you how loved you are. We cannot express our gratitude for your bravery. On this side of the veil we know your true nature. What magnificent souls you are! We also know you have forgotten who you are. It is time for you to awaken and remember your loving greatness. With honor and dignity you have chosen to transform the pains of the Earth. You have heard the cries of pain and anguish from your fellow humans. You yourself have tasted the agony of pain. Underneath your pain lies your ability and greatness.

We are the Counsel.

We have been sent here to help you remember who you are. It is no accident that you are reading this. It is not a coincidence. Find who you are as you read and feel your heart. Go beyond your thinking and feel that quiet place in your soul. Does it pound right now? It pounds because you know on some level, deep inside where you may have forgotten, that this is your calling. It is time for your awakening. The time for the Light Warrior is now. The universe would like to thank you for your undying love in this task. We ask that you gather together and create unity. Show the world what its potential is.

* * * * *

*Soldiers of Light, gather together.*
*Honor us by your presence to all.*
*Show us the peace that is in the heavens.*
*Lead us to the place of grace in our soul.*

* * * * *

The Counsel welcomes you.

Gather yourselves together. Ask for your angel to be with you. Ask for your guide to be with you. Ask the Beginning Without End to be with you while you are presented with this information. Feel your heart. Go inside and feel your empowerment happen. You are honored and loved for your work. Many come and tell you who you are not. Many come and ridicule you because they are afraid of you. You are the light of the world and they know it. Let your light manifest, your gentleness and love. You are a Warrior of the Light. Peace be to you in your fullness.

Today all of the Counsel of Light speaks.

I am the Knowing. I welcome all warriors into this space of learning. I honor and bow to you for the opportunity to present you with your enlightenment. Today we discuss what a Light Warrior is and how you can manifest that part of you. First we must define what a Light Warrior is, and this is my task. The Light Warriors are beings who have incarnated into this earthly realm to help bring in the age of newness, and to help rid the world of the lies that poison the soul. Light Warriors have chosen to be here to unite the world in oneness. This is no small task considering how much uniting there is not. In order to examine the way of the warrior, we must start from his birth.

Before warriors are born, they are told of a wonderful task that needs to be done on the Earth. They are asked whether they would like to help with this task. Each warrior is asked and agrees to do a specific task because he or she is the best suited being for the job. There is nothing warriors would rather do than their tasks. The Beginning Without End has spent much time knowing you and knows what you must learn and what you can teach others. With the knowledge of what you can learn, teach, and help manifest, you and your counsel agree to accept the task. The warrior is very excited and eager to do his job.

It is important to note that the warrior is a highly awakened soul. Warriors are chosen for their advanced ability because earthly ills are not easy to heal and require very spiritually awakened people to do the work. This is important because the warrior does not immediately remember who he is or why he is here.

The perfect parents and life circumstances that aid the warrior's learning are found. After the warrior's earthly life has been established according to his task, the warrior is born at the exact time, on the exact day, to the exact parents, and in the exact bodily form (male or female) required for the learning. When the warrior enters his earthly vessel (his body), his awareness of who he truly is, or his "essence self," slowly is forgotten.

The reason the warrior's memory is erased is because when he comes into the earthly realm, there are several things he needs to accomplish. The first is the required learning. If the warrior came in with knowledge of his full self, there would be no ability to learn the lesson. This is the first journey into the advancement of the warrior's soul. You have your abilities with you right now. You just don't remember them because it is not time to use them. They will not manifest until you have learned the lesson and started your personal task of healing. Healing releases your essence self and enables your remembering.

I am the Truth.

It is important to always remember that only the warrior's memory of his light beingness is forgotten, not his abilities. Understand that the forgetting is only to help the warrior learn. Your light being has never left you. You have merely forgotten how to incorporate it with your physical life, while in your human experience. What then is the first lesson for the warrior? It is how it feels to have all your ability taken away from you, to no longer have your fullness. As an infant, you cannot speak, move, talk, or remember. You are squeezed into a tiny body. If this happened to you right now, most likely you would be helpless and scared. This is why it takes an advanced soul to be a warrior. It is very painful to even be born. You are helpless and dependent on your parents who will help you fulfill the task that you chose to heal, love, and teach about.

There can be more than one task you came to heal. When you are a baby, you can feel your warriorship. However, as you grow and experience your lessons, often they are so painful that you begin to forget why you were born. Often the pain is overwhelming. Some warriors have been put through unbelievable agony. No one can address your task better than you.

The Beginning Without End has chosen you for your unique task because it takes a warrior of very advanced abilities to accomplish its healing. Your bravery in doing this is more than you know or remember. You now know why you are so honored here, so respected, so loved. The Counsel wishes to say that it is we who bow at your feet in love and honor.

During the warrior's early childhood, when he is quiet in his soul, the sacred remembering comes. Sacred remembering is a very private occurrence. It is felt in the deepest part of your soul, in the quiet hours of the day or night. As a child, maybe you would think something like: "There is something great, really great, that I'm here for, but what is it?" You could feel the power in it and revel in the fantasy of it, but you couldn't remember. Later, in adolescence, you were asked: "What do you want to be when you grow up?" You didn't know. There was no name for it. If you could have said: "When I grow up I'm going to be something really great, very special, and it is important for the whole world, but I don't know what it is," that would have been the truth.

In your teen years, you spent a lot of time trying to fit in. No one your age was where you were spiritually, and you didn't feel comfortable talking about it. Often you felt embarrassed, humiliated, ashamed, or unworthy. You spent much time alone. You found that you could relate to adults better, but they told you to play with children your own age. You felt intense aloneness and a great longing in your heart to fit in somewhere.

At this point many warriors turn to drugs, alcohol, or sex to try and alleviate some of their trauma. And every now and then, as you lay awake at night, you would remember the feeling of there being something really big and important you were supposed to do. Still, you couldn't remember what it was. You could feel it, only now your feeling of unworthiness overshadowed your soul. You could not remember who you were.

As the warrior reached adulthood, the question again arose: "What do you want to be when you grow up?" Still, the answer eluded you. You picked a career but you never felt satisfied. Still you heard the whisper: "I am bound to do something great, *but what is it*?" The feeling gnawed at you. You felt frustrated, still searching, still not fitting in. "Where is my task? What is it? When is it my turn? Why am I here?" After much frustration, you buried your longing deep inside. You put up a big wall to hide your warriorship, your true light, to stop it from haunting you.

You now spend your life hiding yourself. Other warriors can see your greatness, but you can't. You use money, power, prestige, clothes, sex, drugs, alcohol, intimidation – anything to disguise your embarrassment, humiliation, shame, and unworthiness, and that haunting feeling of not being able to remember. Blessed are you to have endured this pain to help the world. Let the truth come forward *now*.

Stop and feel yourself right now. You are bound for greatness, something more than money and fame. You, my warrior friends, carry the Great Awakening of Light Warriors. Dare to go back and listen to that voice inside. Feel what it is telling you. It does not care about race, age, or sex. Just for a moment, in the privacy of your mind, ask yourself: "Is there something great I'm supposed to do?" Let the sacred remembering fill your heart. If you know nothing else, know that you are a Warrior of Light. Even if you believe all those lies of embarrassment, humiliation, shame, and unworthiness, feel the warrior hidden in the deepest alcoves of your soul. Know that deep inside you is a mighty being of light that can – and wants to – help the world awaken. Remember who you are. The guides and angels that are with you know that the Beginning Without End chose you. Try and feel the grace of that. You were chosen because you are the best person for the job. You were chosen by the mightiest of divine love to help awaken the world.

We are the Counsel who honor your presence among us. We are here to awaken the Warriors of the Light. That is our task. In doing so, we wish to tell you that you are loved and honored above all warriors. You have bravery in just being born. You have the love of the Beginning Without End in your heart to have endured the pain and suffering of being here. We know of your suffering, warriors. You are honored in the hall of greatness for your endurance. Peace be to you and your remembering.

* * * * *

*I walk the path.*
*There are no directions.*
*No place to go.*
*No map to follow.*
*I walk with the Creator.*
*I need nothing else.*

* * * * *

LESSON FOUR:

# The Warrior's Role

We are the Counsel of Light.

We are the network system for the Beginning Without End. We use "network" because that is the closest word we have to describe our purpose.

There are many of you working on the earth at this time. "Light Warriors" is what we call you. It is the awakening time for Light Warriors and there are many of you remembering your tasks. The Earth is in crisis and is awakening. It needs all the warriors to remember their tasks. We are asking all Light Warriors to gather together and unite the universe in oneness and the divine love of the Beginning Without End. We have been sent here to help guide you on your journey.

Please be aware of the upcoming disasters in the world. Even though they may not affect you physically, they affect the whole world and especially the warriors' energy. The disasters are causing a universal mind consciousness of fear, violence, and hopelessness. The number of people experiencing this mind consciousness is growing faster than the number of warriors awakening to create the mind consciousness of love, unity, and at-oneness needed to awaken into the age of newness.

You have watched the dear souls who cannot hear the messages. You have seen their pain from not being able to connect. They are violent because they do not know how to get out of their pain and connect to their light being, the true essence of who they are. They are like frightened animals. When an animal is afraid, it runs away to a safe place. If there is no safe place for the animal to run, out of fear, it becomes violent trying to protect itself. It is the same with humans.

In order to bring harmony to the rampant violence and fear, the warrior must emanate the light within, the loving light that heals all. The warrior must emanate enough light – the light of divine love – that fear, violence, and distrust in the world give way to love, which in turn creates healing. If we can work together to create oneness and unity on the earth, there will be a time of peace and harmony never before known on your planet.

The most effective way to emanate light is to allow your connectedness to the Beginning Without End to flow through your entire being and emerge so it can be seen and assimilated. The Counsel calls God "the Beginning Without End." We use this term because it includes all spiritual beliefs. You may use any method to create that relationship to the Beginning Without End: however, that relationship is imperative before the Earth's awakening accelerates.

It is important to understand that the coming changes are interrelated on many levels and dimensions. This means that even though you can't see physically what is happening, on an energetic level you can feel what is happening. The effect of these changes is also synergistic. In other words, the total effect is greater than the sum of the individual effects. The combined energy generated by the fear, violence, and hopelessness in the world is greater than the energy of each individual. Likewise, the combined effect of the energy generated by the awakening of many Light Warriors is greater than that which can be generated by each one alone. More important, that combined energy can help negate the effect of those with the mind consciousness of fear, violence, and hopelessness and create a safe place within which to heal.

Just as it is customary for people to help each other in times of trouble, we must see that we are one globe and that everyone is our neighbor. Most of you already know this lesson. Those of you with love in your heart practice it. What you don't know is how many people are aware of compassionate living but don't pay attention to it. People don't necessarily have to be generating disunity to have an impact. If you do nothing, that still is a decision. Those who ignore their role in the world also play a part in its outcome. What role do you play?

The imbalance in numbers may be likened to the situation during the Oklahoma City bombing. There were more injured than doctors, firemen, ambulances and drivers. Nurses, Doctors and emergency medical technicians worked constantly until everyone was cared for. The awakening of the Earth is no different than the bombing of that city. Be assured that there are not enough leaders, teachers, healers, lovers, and intuits addressing the needs of the "bomb site" of the Earth, especially if they only work occasionally.

On a universal scale people are experiencing a disaster of the soul. In order to aid and heal them, the warrior must be at the bomb site day and night until all souls find the warrior within themselves.

The practice of prayer and meditation is imperative. It is how warriors can emanate their light to those at the "bomb site." You must learn to pray together. Praying is synergistic. There is more strength when you pray together and work with each other. It helps the world and you as individuals. Chant together. Meditate together. Do not let yourselves go unheard. Share your prayers with each other so you can accomplish your tasks together.

Don't forget to pray for yourselves. What do you need? What do you want? How can your prayers be answered if you do not go inside yourself and ask for what it is you truly want?

If you cannot give money, give prayers. If you cannot give physical labor, give chants, prayers, and meditations. If you cannot give food, then pray, chant, and meditate. Just because you cannot see the results with your naked eye does not mean there are no results. In fact, prayers, chants and meditations give *the best results*, for you and the world!

"Don't worry," says the Beginning Without End, "I will not leave my workers hungry, tired, harmed, or lost. I have sent you here to help your brothers and sisters. Whatever you need I shall give to you. I am the Red Cross in your heart. Find what your purpose is and do it. When you are tired, rest. When you are hungry, eat. When you need something, ask and I shall give it to you to help you accomplish this task I have sent you to do. Asking helps you to remember self-care and to pay attention to your needs."

"The subject is faith. Where is your faith? First, you must align with your purpose and feel your intention. Then you must feel that you and I are one. I am never away from you. When you sleep, I'm there. When you're awake, working, it doesn't matter, I'm there. If you and I are at 'oneness,' you carry me in your soul."

* * * * *

*From the center core of darkness*
*to the light within*
*there is but one path,*
*one direction,*
*one place of resting.*

*Find the darkness and*
*give it the one light,*
*the one love,*
*the one experience of at-oneness.*

*Then you have led the soul*
*to the place of peace and resting.*

*Create your place of resting in your soul.*
*Through creating, you are showing others*
*the place of resting, peace, and love.*
*Then show them how to carry it always.*

* * * * *

## Lesson Five:
# The Importance of Your Personal Healing

We are the Counsel of Light.

We are delighted to have you among us. It is no coincidence that we are here together. We cannot fully express to you how important your task is to the universe, nor fully express your bravery in being here to complete the task you have agreed upon. Today, with the divine essence of love, the Counsel gathers together to tell you of the future of your planet. It is necessary at this point to say that the outcome of your planet depends on your work as Light Warriors. There are a great many ills to heal before unity can take place. If you gather together and unite, you can heal and awaken the planet – and that is your task. It is a multifaceted task. Since the universe is holographic, everything is interconnected, and healing takes place at every level for everyone. By the same token, so does abuse. We will explain this to try and show the importance of your personal healing to you as well as to the whole.

We shall use the example of an evening at the symphony orchestra. When we look at an orchestra we can see there are many different instruments. We marvel at them all. We may personally like one instrument better than another; however, we see them all as wonderful makers of music. After we, as the audience, are seated, we anticipate the concert of instruments with much joy and excitement. We are awaiting the conductor. As the musicians take to the stage, each picks up his instrument. Each musician loves the instrument he chooses to play. More importantly, the musician's deepest desire is to play that instrument. Nothing else in his life makes him more happy. You can see it on his face.

The musicians also see each other with respect. Each musician sees the other as having worked very hard to learn to play the instrument of his desire. Each musician can look at the others and, without doubt or hesitation, understand the love that the other musicians have for their chosen instruments. Because they understand how much love, work, and desire it takes to learn to play an instrument, they develop respect for each other and see each other as comrades and equals. They also know that to create one piece of music, they must unite their individual sounds into one. The musician does not say that his is the most important sound. Rather, the musician understands that his instrument must be played or the symphony will not be whole. There will be a piece missing. The audience and the musician will know that an instrument is missing and this will create a lack of wholeness in the audience and in the musicians.

When the conductor arrives, he gives each section of instruments a part to play – notes on a page to create a harmony of sound, the joyous sound of harmony in unity. The conductor loves all the instruments equally. He knows of each one's importance. He knows that to have unity of sound, he must have all the instruments together. He understands the musicians' love of music. The conductor chose each and every musician for his outstanding ability to play his instrument. He understands the dedication, hard work, pain, and long hours they put in to have achieved that state of excellence. He is proud of his musicians. The conductor knows the uniqueness of each instrument, but he also knows that the sounds are interconnected to create one sound. His job is to create the unison and harmony of all the instruments playing together.

The people in the audience have faith that the conductor picked the best musicians and are eager to hear them play. They need to hear the music. It helps bring love and joy to their soul. They bought tickets in advance, and after a hard day of work they are looking forward to listening to the symphony. They are in their seats and the soft whispers of excited people can be heard. As the lights dim slowly, the excitement builds, and yet it is so quiet you could hear a pin drop. The musicians are in their places waiting for the conductor to lead them. As he walks onto the stage, the audience breaks into applause. The conductor bows and you can see the love, pride, and joy on his face. Everyone knows he has picked the best musicians. He loves the audience and wants to help them relax and feel good, and experience the unity in the sound of his orchestra.

The conductor lifts his baton and the musicians gather together and wait for the signal to start playing. The conductor begins and the musicians start to play. They are not envious of each other's parts. Each loves his part and knows how important it is to play his individual melody. As the room fills with the sweet sound of music, the audience begins to feel harmony, wonderful love, and joy – such good feelings. The pressures of the day fall away, and the love of listening to music fills their souls and rejuvenates their hearts. Peace has been created by the unity of sound. The joy of the music becomes so great it brings tears to their eyes. Some people are so moved that they cry quietly. Somehow, the whole room is lifted to a "higher state of being." Everyone becomes connected with one another. Audience and orchestra experience at-oneness. Ahhh! Such communion!

After the concert, there is great applause, joy, and thankfulness. The audience rises to its feet. "*Bravo, Bravo!!*" shouts the crowd in thanks and appreciation for the sound of unity. The audience leaves feeling relaxed, joyous, happy and full of love. When they step out of the auditorium into the world, they now are giving out the new energy from a wonderful night full of love and unity. When the audience leaves, much respect and honor is given to the musicians, and there is thankfulness for the peace in their souls created by the music.

You see my young warriors, it is a big, honorable task that you have. You are the musicians playing the instruments. The conductor is the Beginning Without End. The whole universe is the audience. Not just the Earth. The Earth is but a grain of sand on a beach, only one planet. The rest of the beach is the universe. The universe is awaiting the concert of the planet Earth. The concert must include and unify everyone. When the music is heard by the universe, if it is all together, it will have the same healing effect on the audience as it has on the orchestra. This couldn't be more important. The one sound the Earth makes will create unity on the planet and in the universe. You can believe that the whole universe is watching, waiting with anticipation and excitement. The music the Earth makes can unify the universe because it is holographic. We are all interconnected. We are all created by the same Creator.

What happens in regard to Earth changes on your planet depends upon the work being done now. Many talk about how the Earth will shake and many other possibilities that leave the warrior frightened. The warrior begins to become so afraid he turns into a survivalist. He becomes the violent animal we spoke of earlier.

There is hope. The power to create a new awakening on the Earth is in the hands of the Warriors of the Light. You must find your instrument and join the orchestra in making the harmonious sound to unite the universe in oneness. By accepting your warriorship, you have the ability to help unite the Earth and the universe forever in love and oneness through the Beginning Without End. That is the great change of the Earth spoken of so often. If you, new warrior, want to play your instrument, you must pull it out of its case and warm up. Your instrument is inside you. You have always had it with you and have spent your entire life learning to play it. To learn to open the case and bring your instrument out is what the Counsel will teach you.

You must know that playing the instrument is your deepest longing. Your will and the conductor's will are the same. Warriors, that is to say that your will and the will of the Beginning Without End are the same. You both desire and love the same thing. Both of you want to work together to make the same music. You don't give up anything when you align with your warriorship. You only give up the confusion within yourself. In playing your instrument you will create oneness in yourself, your family lineage, the Earth, and the universe. You see, there is greatness in this. We shall teach you the basic tools to tap into your instrument. We shall help you unite with other Warriors of the Light. We shall show the warrior how to have abundance in his earthly and spiritual life.

This is the age of newness – new life, new ways of living, new ways of thinking and communicating – all full of the possibility of living to the fullness the Beginning Without End intended for us all. It is with great excitement that the Counsel has spoken about this. We share in your excitement of oneness. We pray for you Light Warriors to help you find your instruments. It is in honor and love that we move to the next lesson.

*   *   *   *   *

*In unity with the conductor,*
*all is possible.*
*All is within.*
*All is in all is in one.*

*   *   *   *   *

## Lesson Six:
# Understanding Belief Systems

Good morning. I am the Voice.

I am the voice that is within you. I am the sound of oneness. I am the tone of the Beginning Without End. I am the sound of awakening. The Voice will teach about the poisoning of the soul. I also want to address the antidote.

Since you have committed yourself to finding your greatness and helping bring in the age of newness, you must know of the poisons that affect your life, and the lives of other warriors. The poisons are beliefs that are blocking the true self. Some of these blocks feel so big or deep that some warriors can neither find themselves, nor do they wish to. Instead, they wish to hide themselves. The warrior becomes afraid that these beliefs, which he learns as a child, are actually true. The warrior who blocks the true self has a hard time finding his path. He has a hard time connecting with his task, and becomes unhappy in the life presently being lived. After much time has gone by, the warrior has lost himself and settles into a "whatever" life, never really being truly happy.

The true poison however, is not that the warrior never manifests, because that is always possible. The greater sadness is that this warrior crosses to the other side without realizing his core self and misses the opportunity to share his greatness with other warriors and the world. The warrior dies without finding the personal truth that was for his advancement. This is a tragedy.

Let us examine some of these belief systems now. We shall use a belief system that plagues many warriors: the "You will amount to nothing" belief system. When the warrior is first told he will amount to nothing (usually by his caregivers), it drives a deep pain into his heart. The warrior feels as though his parents are embarrassed, humiliated, and shamed by him. The warrior also feels embarrassed, humiliated, shamed, and not very lovable or important.

Many things may happen then. First, the warrior child will want to please his parents and try to show them that he is someone worthwhile, that he is lovable. He will do whatever it takes to show them he is worthy of their respect. But the parents continue to tell the young warrior that he will not amount to anything. The warrior feels he is failing in his attempts to show them he is worthy and *will* amount to something. After several attempts to try and gain balance with his parents, the warrior starts to believe their statements. The warrior will then start to either *dissolve* the statement or *emanate* the statement that has been attributed to him.

The warrior who tries to *dissolve* that statement will become an over-achiever, striving for greatness at work, at home, through the acquisition of material possessions, and by maintaining a high standard of living. The warrior is trying to disprove the belief system that exists in the family and in himself. He may believe that he is healing his family by picking things that prove he amounts to something rather than picking things that make him happy. He will try and prove to his parents, supervisors, and colleagues that he amounts to something. He also has to try and stop the haunting sound of his soul's calling.

The warrior will try and prove that he is worthy to his spouse. He may even pick his spouse because the partner truly believes in the warrior and feels that he is special. This adoration by the spouse becomes confirmation for the warrior of his value and potential. The warrior builds an illusion of who he is by the people and things with which he surrounds himself.

But the warrior still is haunted with doubt. Inside, he still believes he is not good enough and is nothing. He feels as though he hasn't done enough to prove that he amounts to something. He may even give himself a pep talk about how to achieve more greatness, or what he could do better to dissolve his self-doubt.

His greatest fear is that someone may find out what he believes about himself and verify it. He also is afraid to lose his possessions, his job, his lifestyle, or anything that helps keep that belief hidden from the world and himself.

The warrior keeps waiting for his parents to say how proud of him they are, to accept him and value him. However, they always seem to remind him of his shortcomings. It feels as though they never say anything supportive to him. Maybe there is a brother or sister that he feels has more approval or favor with his parents. It seems that no matter what, he never quite measures up in their eyes and therefore in his own. The warrior may take to drinking, sex, or religion to hide the pain.

Years of this type of internal conflict create undue stress on the body and mind. The stress of the belief system eventually manifests itself as illness. For example, the stress of keeping up appearances may cause a heart attack, high blood pressure, cancer, or other diseases.

The warrior now has spent his whole life trying to disprove a statement made to him in his childhood. This is what has been called "the wound." He never finds his gift or his purpose.

How does this affect his relationships? He may demand that all his friends respect him. In his own mind he may be good at everything and know the most. He may be competitive at work, always trying to be the top person. He may be a perfectionist. He will want all of his colleagues to look to him for answers. If he is in a leadership position, his standards for the people he leads may be very high. He may want his team to shine – to be the best – not because they are the best, but because it will prove, once again, that he amounts to something. Those people on his team may be replaced or chastised for not living up to his standards. This gives him a false sense of superiority, reinforcing the belief that he is amounting to something.

However, this facade is a fragile one. If his bosses want more from him, they have only to make statements like, "You have done such a great job leading, *but* . . . ," or, "We have noticed that you're working very hard, but you could certainly do better *if* . . . ." He never really is praised for his diligence and hard work. His superiors know of his belief system and can manipulate him with it. They know because they suffer from the same beliefs. This is very important to realize, warrior one. How are you manipulated by your belief systems?

How does this affect his marriage? He may have picked a spouse that looks up to him. This person truly knows his greatness. He, however, thinks he has hidden who he believes he truly is away deep enough that no one will ever see it. He may even speak about it to his spouse. He may say things like, "My family always thought my sibling was better than me." Or, "I'm the black sheep of my family, the rebel." He may share with his spouse a little of the pain caused by the childhood injury. He may not even know that he also believes what was told to him in his early years.

The spouse may unknowingly say something that triggers this belief system and sets off those awful feelings again – something like, “Honey, I think we might have done better at that *if* . . . .” This in turn may set off an argument. The partner has unintentionally triggered the uncomfortable feelings of inadequacy from which the warrior has worked so hard to hide. Some warriors actually leave their marriages because they think their partners no longer believe they are going to amount to anything.

What is worse is if the partner begins to be more successful than the warrior. The warrior’s belief system will kick right in and he may not even feel worthy of his spouse. He may start to belittle his partner in order to feel better and instead start the downfall of his own marriage. He then perpetuates what he learned as a child. This is the greatest tragedy – when the soul is so lost it perpetuates its own poisoning.

With this example, we can see how the warrior slowly forgets and hides his true greatness. The warrior is lost in trying to “fix” himself. The warrior could not find the self hidden in the lie of the belief system.

These types of belief systems are very manipulative. They allow other people and things to control you. Your soul and your creativity are imprisoned. Your world task is locked up behind the bars of illusion. This is the poisoning of the soul.

When the warrior’s essence is imprisoned by a belief system, his personal task is to shatter that illusional prison cell. This heals not only the warrior, but the warrior’s predecessors and future generations of warriors. This is the antidote. If you can neutralize the poison in you, then you have transformed it so as not to be passed on to your children warriors, and you have healed it in other warriors and in the world. It is all interconnected.

Let us now look at an example of the behavior of a warrior who *emanates* the same belief system. Again, the first time the warrior hears "You will not amount to anything," it causes deep pain in his soul. This statement reflects the wounding of his soul. The warrior feels his parents are embarrassed, humiliated, and shamed by him. The pain is so great in this warrior that he shuts down inside. He does not talk to other people and is picked on by other children. This serves to reinforce his pain. He spends a lot of time fantasizing about things that make him a hero that everyone can be proud of. This warrior watches a lot of television so he can ignore how awful he feels inside. TV becomes an escape, and sometimes the warrior may even have good feelings from a certain show, or from seeing his favorite hero win over the "bad guys."

When he gets to high school, the young warrior is failing school and does not know how to relate to people. This warrior is drowning in the belief that he will not amount to anything. But unlike in the first example, he is not going to do anything to try to erase that belief; rather, he will emanate it. In later years, if he finds a partner it doesn't matter to him how badly the partner treats him. The warrior believes he is lucky to even have someone notice him. Furthermore, the warrior feels that he deserves to be mistreated because he "is not going to amount to anything" anyway, and he truly believes he is awful. This warrior will do anything to keep the partner happy because he truly believes that this is the only partner who would ever want him. He can be manipulated into anything.

This warrior has problems with drugs and alcohol at the high school age. He doesn't go to college, nor does he dream of going. These warriors often find work in minimum wage jobs and stay there, feeling afraid to try something else because they "aren't good enough." They fantasize about greatness and are creative with many exceptional ideas, but they can never bring them to fruition. Usually these warriors are excellent artists, musicians, or painters. They are very passionate people but keep their passion hidden because it has been a source of taunting for them. They are sensitive and loving, but they hide it.

This warrior also has a lot of sacred remembering but trivializes it. He has many late nights of feeling his soul call to him and of listening to the whispers of greatness. Yet he dismisses these callings because he truly believes he will not amount to anything. Every time he has a great idea, the warrior dismisses it as something that will be done by someone who is "better."

This warrior often lives in mental and material poverty. He does not talk very much and mostly just observes people. He is secretly afraid people would mistreat him if they found out how awful he was.

The warrior with this type of injury is the most sensitive. He has a lot of *déjà vu*, and during sleep his dreams are very vivid. It's as though the sacred remembering is trying to speak to him even when he is sleeping (and it is). This warrior feels haunted by the sacred remembering, yet trapped by the belief system that tells him he will not amount to anything. Again we can see how this warrior is imprisoned by the belief system.

We shall make note here that there is a difference in the way each warrior has been imprisoned, even though warriors may have the same belief systems. This is because each warrior was born with her own personal task to heal. The warrior was chosen for her abilities to heal that family's lineage. Each lineage has its own unique imbalance. It has belief systems that have imprisoned that family for generations. The warrior born into that lineage is chosen for her ability to heal it. Maybe the warrior was chosen for her strength or love or patience. Maybe she was chosen because she has the tenacity and attentiveness to complete the task no warrior before her had been able to clear away.

A good example of someone who conquered a belief system and had fruition of her world task is Harriet Tubman. We shall look at this heroine's belief systems, her sacred awakening, and her personal and world tasks. She is an excellent example of the antidote to the illusional prison you warriors have come here to shatter. Her experience shows you how to dissolve the lies and poison that stop many warriors from achieving their tasks. We also shall see how she created unity between herself and God, as well as among those she helped.

Harriet Tubman started the underground railroad, a secret escape route out of the American South for slaves. She personally freed approximately 70,000 slaves. Harriet was also a nurse, a scout, and a spy during the Civil War. She was born with the task of leading America into the new age of freedom. She was chosen because she was the best warrior for that job. In order to heal the world of several belief systems, she personally had to experience the pain of them, listen to her sacred awakening, find her connection to the Beginning Without End, dissolve the belief system within herself (her personal task, freeing herself), and complete her world task (freeing other slaves). (Harriet called the Beginning Without End "God," so we shall use that term in this section.)

The belief systems of that period kept many men enslaved. It was believed that men and women of color should be bought and sold into slavery. Some of the belief systems of that time were: "blacks should be slaves"; "blacks that can't read or write aren't smart enough to free themselves"; "blacks don't deserve to be free"; "if you are a freed slave, no one will help you"; "you won't find work if you free yourself"; and "it's OK to brutalize and abuse slaves."

These beliefs kept many slaves from trying to escape their horrible conditions. Many who were born into slavery believed there was no other way of life, that there was no hope of being free and you were crazy if you tried to escape. Capture meant excruciating punishment or death. Those slaves who escaped and were caught were often made examples of.

Many slaves called Harriet the "Black Moses." The Counsel prefers to call her a "Light Warrior." She was born into slavery and her owners were very brutal, beating her nearly every day. Her owner was a religious woman but didn't have the true presence of God in her heart because she still saw fit to beat her slave. Harriet prayed to God to make her a strong woman, able to withstand the horrible abuse. At one point, Harriet suffered a head injury from a weight thrown at another slave by her master. It hit Harriet instead, causing a brain disease that was very severe for a long time.

Even though she was in the worst of earthly conditions, at night she too had her sacred awakening. She heard that voice that spoke to the deepest part of her soul. She did not ignore or trivialize this connection. She knew it was God. She felt the presence of God speaking to her. She let that presence empower her soul and rejuvenate her spirit. Harriet *felt*. She had no books, radio, or television to distract her. She just felt the presence of God.

Not ignoring that powerful voice within is the most important piece of the warrior's puzzle. Many warriors have the sacred awakening but feel unworthy of the presence of the Creator. They get stuck in the poison of the soul and feel unworthy, and so they disconnect themselves from the sacred awakening.

Harriet felt the fear, pain, and anguish of watching her people be mistreated, beaten, raped, and tortured because they were slaves. She had endured the same horrible abuse. She was born into slavery so she could learn about and experience this horrible condition. She agreed to this task before she incarnated but her memory was erased to facilitate the learning. Harriet was chosen because she was the best warrior for this job. But she had to find the warrior within to help lead her people. She did not lose herself in her pain or fear. She had to overcome the challenges of being black, being a slave and a woman, being unable to read, having no money, and being afraid of being caught.

Harriet's closest companion was God. She prayed to be strong and able to fight. When she prayed to God he answered her prayers right then, but she had to learn to trust and listen to God's voice within her giving her directions and telling her who to trust. This woman could not even read the "Wanted Dead or Alive" posters with her picture on them.

After the learning, she began her personal task of dissolving the belief systems that plagued her. This was her healing. Harriet wanted her brothers to run away with her, but they didn't agree and vigorously tried to talk her out of it. They were trapped in the same belief systems that poison the soul. They may have said things to her like, "Harriet, you're not going to make it" or "They will beat you and kill you." They may have tried to discourage her by telling her that she wasn't strong enough or that she would not have enough food and would surely die in the wilderness. She had no money, and even if she had money, there were no grocery stores or restaurants for her to go to.

You see, she had to dissolve those belief systems in herself first, because in order to lead other slaves to freedom, she would have to show them how to dissolve those belief systems in themselves. She had to experience her own pain in order to help other slaves resolve their fears so they, too, could become free. She knew what to say to them to comfort them or to confront them. She was able to inspire them through the example of her own experience.

Since there were no therapists or healers to help her dissolve those belief systems, she used prayer and meditation to overcome them. She communed with God to help her listen to the voice within. Then one day, she walked off into the forest and was free, alone with God as her guide.

Having completed her personal task, Harriet's world task became the rest of her life. She was the greatest female abolitionist in history. She died in 1913 having fully realized her warriorship and completed her task of bringing in the new age of freedom. She showed others how to touch the face of God.

A paragraph in the March, 1865 edition of *The Freemen's Record* beautifully describes Harriet's faith. "When going on journeys Harriet often lay alone in the forest all night. Her whole soul was filled with awe of the mysterious Unseen Presence, which thrilled her with such depths of emotion, that all other care and fear vanished. Then she seemed to speak with her maker, as a man talketh with his friend; her child-like petitions had direct answers, and beautiful visions lifted her up above all doubt and anxiety into serene trust and faith. No man can be a hero without this faith in some form, the sense that he walks not in his own strength, but leaning on an almighty arm. Call it fate, destiny, call it what you will, Moses of old, Moses of today, believed it to be Almighty God."

This is the antidote to the poison of the soul. What do you think would have happened if Harriet had not listened to her sacred awakening? How might the world be now? How many people is her legacy still enriching?

Can you feel the warrior in your own soul? Take a moment and feel your empowerment!

Each warrior is born to learn about the belief systems that imprison both his lineage and the warrior himself. Some belief systems are individual and some are worldwide. For example, the race culture you were born into has its unique belief systems. Likewise, different countries have their own individual and world belief systems.

Take some time right now and try to write down what you think are some of your personal and family belief systems. Try to see how you are manipulated by these belief systems. Can you see the illusionary prison you are in?

Now, take some time and feel the heart area in your body. Ask your guides or angels to help you feel that sacred place of awakening. If you feel the poison of the soul creep in, ask your guide to quiet that feeling. You must *feel* the sacred awakening in your soul. It is a knowing, a deep longing that radiates greatness. For many warriors, simply reading these words is creating the light in their soul. It is no accident that this happens. It is you, mighty Light Warrior, who we have come to awaken.

There are many great Light Warriors still alive today. Former U.S. President Jimmy Carter is a modern day warrior. He was a farmer's son born in the small town of Plains, Georgia. He went to public schools and then served in the Navy. He resigned from his naval career when his father died and returned home to Georgia to work on the farm.

Carter eventually became interested in public affairs in his community. He first was appointed chairman of the local school board, and then in 1962 he won election to the Georgia

Senate. Later, he became the 76th Governor of Georgia, and in 1976 he was elected President of the United States.

It would seem that this great warrior had accomplished his world task after being president. However, Carter knew his warriorship did not end there. After helping to implement some of the greatest diplomatic treaties of the present era, he wrote 12 books, founded the Carter Center, started a community resource program called The Atlanta Project and turned it into a national program called The America Project; and he still manages to roll up his sleeves and provide labor for Habitat for Humanity. He also is a deacon in his church and teaches Sunday school. You can see that this warrior contributed greatly in many different areas. He still is doing so today.

Note here, dear warrior, that these people lived abundant lives while doing their world tasks. These warriors were well taken care of by the universe. For example, President Carter lived in absolute luxury while doing his purpose. Abundance exists in the world, and the Beginning Without End will provide for you.

We each may not be able to accomplish as many things as Jimmy Carter, but we should recognize that our work can be every bit as satisfying and abundant.

These warriors of yesterday and today are excellent examples. Both had their sacred awakenings. Both had challenges and belief systems to overcome. Dear warriors, know that you also have this greatness in you. These warriors had big, wonderful tasks, and so do you. Both of these warriors brought things that were not yet present on the planet. What they brought came from within them.

It is with much honor and dignity that the Counsel of Light praises and thanks you for the opportunity to bring you this lesson. Our prayer is that you find your true nature and path.

*     *     *     *     *

*I feel the burning in my soul;*
*there is nothing that puts out the fire.*
*I feel the answer in my soul;*
*there is nothing that puts out the fire.*
*I feel the connection to the Creator;*
*that is the fire.*

*     *     *     *     *

## Lesson Seven:
# Setting Intention for Your Warriorship

---

I am the Truth.

I welcome and honor your presence for the learning and the healing of your planet. The greatness of your bravery for being here on the planet at this time is not measurable nor can we express it in words, for there are no words to express it. You are so loved, warriors. Our love for you knows no bounds. We honor your work with unconditional, divine love that the Beginning Without End has blessed us with. Your awakening is a task that deserves all the love and honor it can have. I am the Truth. We shall start the learning with the lesson of intention.

Many warriors have some knowledge and feeling that there is some great purpose to complete in their lives. They can feel the sacred awakening come alive in them and wonder what next steps they should take as a new warrior. The first is deep inner reflection and prayer. You also must create your intention. What is your intention? You should take entering into your warriorship seriously. You are undertaking a task.

If you are taking a trip to another state you don't just get in your car and drive. You plan your trip with intention. For example, you would give thought to how long you will be gone, where you will stay and who you will be seeing. If you are driving, you need to know how far it is, whether the car is in good condition and how much gas you will need to get there and back. After much preparation, you can begin your trip, and not before.

If it is your intention to answer your soul's Light Warrior expression, self- reflection and prayer are necessary. You may ask the Beginning Without End for guidance because you do not yet know your purpose. That is your quest and now you need help. You have many questions. How will the warrior recognize help when it is sent? Will another warrior help him? Is there another book to read about your purpose? You may never have prayed before. You might need help finding your path.

You may think about what your commitment level is. This is a very big task. Many new warriors must reflect on how much work it is to heal themselves first. Sometimes warriors dissolve the belief systems that imprison them, only to find there are underlying belief systems they didn't before recognize. Where warriors can find help dissolving these belief systems is a question the Counsel will address in a later lesson. For now, know that as a fledgling warrior, the most important thing is to set your intention.

When the warrior has made time for self-reflection and prayer, he can make intention. This should be done in a ceremony accepting your warriorship. It is cause for celebration and prayer and may include taking a vow to find your true self. A commitment can be made with intention and conviction to help bring in the age of newness and unite the universe in oneness; to help awaken the universe with the sound of your instrument by finding your essence through all the soul poisons. When the vow is made you should have something to wear on your person to remind you that you are a Light Warrior and have made a commitment, perhaps a ring or necklace or crystal.

After you have taken your vow, congratulations and a celebration are in order. On this side of the veil we celebrate every time a Light Warrior accepts his task or has his remembering. You have our deepest appreciation. It is important for warriors to gather together in celebration with dignity and feast together and honor each other's tasks. Pray together and work together and by your example show others how to work together.

During the time of self-reflection and making intention, the warrior should look not only at his personal healing but also at what he might be able to do as a result of his work.

One day, the channel and her counsel were watching a television talk show. Two very impressive young warriors – each about 16 years old – were on the show. Both of these young warriors had been born with the personal task of healing their anorexia. They had begun that task at an early age – about 11 years old. They endured incredible suffering, and both had come close to dying. But they both had recovered from their illnesses, and at 16 years old they were teaching the world about this awful disorder. They did not have teaching certificates or psychology degrees, but they knew the disorder intimately and had the true wisdom of surviving and healing. There are no better teachers for that particular job than those two young women. They are true warriors.

An important step each of these warriors took was their determination to get better. They opened the instrument case inside themselves and had deliberate intention to become healthy. They are excellent examples of what it means to have intention.

Your task may not be as difficult or it may be more difficult; however, your intention must be solid. You must take the personal work seriously to get to the world task.

We shall speak of reflection now. Reflection can help you figure out what belief systems are imprisoning your soul. It is good to sit alone quietly and to ask the Beginning Without End to help you gently look at yourself. The warrior may start with simple feelings and should write each down. It is important to write these belief systems down to help your healer help you. (We shall explain in another lesson what help is available to the new warrior.) You may feel tears well up as you write these tender feelings down. Some examples of belief systems are: "I'm not worthy"; "I'm too fat"; "I'm too short"; "I'm too stupid"; "I'm not lovable"; "No one cares for me"; "I never had what my sibling had." Include abuses you may have endured. Perhaps you were sexually assaulted, physically assaulted, ignored, or neglected. Write down any abuse that comes to mind. If you were traumatized by the loss of a loved one, write it down. If you feel tears, let them come down your face and allow your guides and angels to comfort you, my warrior.

This is the pain of the learning. It hurts the soul, but your bravery is immense. By entering into your warriorship, you have chosen to heal your injury so no other warrior will have to endure the suffering and pain you have. It is the most noble expression of your greatness and we on this side of the veil cannot express enough our gratitude and respect for your helping the universe.

When you warriors are reflecting upon your pain, it is most important that you treat yourself with gentleness. You have been told the lies about yourself and are now feeling the pain of the poison. After completing the task of reflecting on your pain, do something that gives you comfort. Treat yourself to something that honors you.

Once you have completed this task, it is time to reflect and write once more. Again, find a quiet spot in a sacred area, a garden, a mountain, a temple, or a peaceful room. Lay down or sit comfortably and quiet your mind. Go inside your heart and recall how you felt each time you had a sacred remembering. Write down in as much detail as you can what you felt, said, heard or thought, the time of day, and all the events surrounding the remembering. Stay in that space for a while and feel the feelings you had about that remembering.

After you have completed that, you must next meditate on your strengths and skills. Return to the same quiet spot and write in detail everything you are good at and everything you love to do. If you have a good memory, or if you are creative, patient, athletic, good at cooking, smart, or tenacious, write it down. Last, write down any physical conditions you have, such as a bad back, asthma, weight problems, a bad heart, attention deficit disorder, epilepsy, or any other physical clue. These, my dear ones, are clues to your task and purpose. These are the hints needed to help you heal those belief systems. As you can see, you have endured a lot of suffering in your lifetime. You have what it takes to heal the lineage. This is why you were chosen to do your task. You are the chosen one. You are the best warrior for your task. Choose to heal those soul poisons in you. When you heal them in you, the bonus is that you also heal them within your lineage.

We are very compassionate about the pain you have suffered. Many of you are still suffering those pains. It is time to find your true self and find your path. Maybe you are the warrior who will write the next book on the pain that you have healed. Maybe you are the warrior who starts the next support group or coalition. Maybe you are the warrior who changes the laws or Constitution to help other warriors rid the world of the pain you endured. Maybe you are the warrior who finds the cure for your illness. Only you have the key, warrior. It is within you.

It is with much love and honor for you that we end this lesson with a prayer for the Light Warriors in their learning.

* * * * *

*Ask and it will be granted.*
*Heal and it shall be so.*
*Find your greatness and*
*manifest the loving bravery*
*that is the symphony of unison.*

*We bow at your feet.*
*We sing your song of praise and love.*
*You have endured suffering to awaken the world.*
*Ask for abundance and it shall be so.*

* * * * *

LESSON EIGHT:

# Dissolving Your Belief Systems

---

We are the Counsel of Light.

Thank you for allowing us into your hearts and minds. Warriors are truly magnificent souls, with immense love in their hearts. We feel your love and presence as you read the lessons. It is with the dignity of the Light Warrior that we present the next lesson.

First, we shall review intention to ensure your alignment with it. Intention is making a cognitive decision to do something that you have made an alignment with. Alignment is the synchronization of your body, feelings, and spiritual being. It is sudden and sharp, and it comes with a lot of conviction. Coming into alignment with your warriorship, the Beginning Without End, and your world task are not small intentions. They are part of the great awakening of your soul. They affect everything and everyone.

This is no small matter and not to be taken lightly. It is as important as the commitment you make in marriage. You are, in a sense, learning to marry yourself first. When you marry, it is because you are certain that the love you have for your partner can withstand the tests of the world. When you accept your warriorship, you are learning to go inside yourself and marry the warrior within you, allowing it to manifest in the world. We usually do not walk out on a marriage because it doesn't feel good – we try to go within the marriage and bring balance to it. It is the same with warriorship. Processing the wounds of the warrior takes bravery, love, and faith.

Aligning with your intention to manifest your healing is the first step. The first alignment is bravery. It means having courage when fear has gripped you or you feel as though you are not worthy of your warriorship. Having the boldness to start the path of warriorship lends its way to fearlessness. This does not mean that fear disappears, but gentleness and bravery manifest and the warrior finds the courage to go beyond her fear. You learn to allow your fear to be present and not to let it stop you. That is to say, you allow it to be there instead of trying to dissolve it or emanate it. You know the fear may be a belief system that you no longer wish to be imprisoned by.

When you begin to align with your warriorship, you will develop first as a young cub. Self-love develops from bravery because we have now started to bring our true essence forward and awaken our love essence. As bravery turns into love, we mature into a lion, the gentle loving king of the jungle that no one will disturb.

When your bravery starts growing into love for yourself, you develop compassion for your fellow warriors. You understand how hard it is for the warrior to emerge. You recognize the bravery it takes each warrior to manifest and so you develop respect for one another. If a warrior gets lost in his pain, you help him with the great task at hand because you understand the difficulty and can help. Bravery gives way to gentleness, love, and compassion in the warrior, both for the self and for other warriors. Mutual respect, friendship, and a sense of community will develop as a result.

The warrior will find through the processing of belief systems that he really is the magnificent soul he dreamed he would be. He learns through going deep inside himself and communing with his guides, counsel, and the Beginning Without End that there truly is a purpose for him. There really is a gift he is supposed to leave with the world. He will learn that his gift and purpose are his deepest, deepest longing. Nothing else will make him more happy in his life than to answer his calling.

Aligning with the intention to manifest your purpose creates optimum health and happiness in the warrior. Love begins to weave faith into the warrior. The warrior realizes that prayer really does work and that she carries her prayer with her always. She knows that all her needs and wants can be addressed and provided for. Suddenly, the warrior will realize that she is living her life from the place of warriorship. She begins hearing her guidance as to where to be, what to do, and with whom to speak, and she has the love, courage, and faith to listen. Life becomes wonderful harmony and magic. It begins to align with the feeling of communion. The warrior yearns for nothing else but to live, work, and love from this place. When you have learned to live in this space of communion, you will have found the age of newness.

* * * * *

*Fear not; fear is afraid also.*
*Take the mask of illusion off.*
*Free yourselves and sit on the throne.*
*You are the kings and queens of the Earth.*

* * * * *

We are the Counsel of Light.

You are the warriors. Yes, you are the souls that are foretold in your books of prophets. The kingdom of peace and love can manifest when the Warrior of Light awakens.

I am the Truth.

It is my honor to serve you as you have served us. Blessings are manyfold for the warrior. Today we start the lesson of awakening, the transformation of the warrior.

First, we shall have a brief discussion on the energy field, what it is and does. The energy field (which is also termed the "aura") is a radiant sphere of energy that interpenetrates and surrounds your body. The energy field has layers that also are called "bodies." As you do your process work and come closer to your essence self, these bodies become clearer and more healthy. This process helps release your soul self or essence self.

Clearing these layers also helps your physical body. Your physical body is dependent on your energy field for health. Energy is gathered through special energy centers called "chakras" within your energy field and is assimilated into your body for use. For more information on the human energy field, please read the book *Hands of Light* by Barbara Ann Brennan.

Now that we have gone over intention, alignment, and your energy field or aura, we can go deeper into awakening, or what takes place during the process of dissolving belief systems.

When we learn a belief system and think it is the truth, we take the belief system and "own" it. We say that it is ours, or we may say, "I am this belief system." When the warrior does this, he has to hide somewhere the truth of who he really is. So, the young warrior pushes his true essence way down in his body to a deep place where no one can get to it. When he does this, he stops the natural flow of energy through his body and energy field. He uses some of the energy intended for his health to keep his essence or true self hidden. This also blocks the energy flow in his energy field. The result of these blockages to the natural flow of energy is to cause imbalance in the life, spiritual, and energy forces of the warrior.

Since the body needs energy flowing through the aura for assimilation and optimum health, we can see how illness steps in the moment energy becomes blocked. It may start as fatigue, and later, if it remains unbalanced, will manifest as a more serious illness. For example, let's say a parent tells the young warrior, "Stop crying, or I'll give you something to cry about." The warrior fears more abuse, so he then squishes his tears somewhere deep inside himself. He also has to push down his true hurt feelings, and his desire and need to cry. This requires a lot of energy at first.

The first time the warrior did this at a young age, it exhausted him and he might have taken a nap. After years of stifling his tears, however, the warrior finds he cannot cry without difficulty and he is used to this. He also has forgotten his essence, which he pushed down. The warrior forgets what his essence even feels like or that he has his essence within him. He takes on many masks and disguises to help keep himself from ever crying. Every time the urge to cry comes up, the warrior has been trained to shove it back down. He does so even if there is no longer the threat of abuse. He has forgotten who he is and will shove himself away again and again. Now his life force, emotional energy, and spiritual energy are being used to imprison him within himself.

How then do we go about rescuing ourselves from this illusional prison? First, we must know that we have imprisoned our essence, and the illusion of pain is the door guard. We also must know that we cannot see our essence with pain blocking the view into the prison cell. You must have faith that your essence *is* in the prison cell. You need to believe that you *are* in that cell and that it is not empty.

When the warrior wishes to free herself, she must first be made aware that she has been conditioned by many occurrences of the same belief system. The warrior has the Pavlov's dog reaction. When the warrior who has been told not to cry feels her pain, she will have the automatic reaction of shoving herself back down. She does this because when she feels pain, she is threatened by that old memory. To that warrior, wanting to cry means more abuse. Even as an adult, when tears are present, it is painful to let them out because she has been trained to associate that emotion with abuse.

This, my dear warrior, is where your bravery comes in. The true warrior has to take back his essence. He must go in the prison cell. He must do what his essence originally wanted. In this example, the warrior needs to cry to see that nothing will happen to him except to feel his feelings. The lie of "more abuse" is over. No one can abuse the adult warrior any more. The warrior can take a look at the belief systems around crying and dissolve these also. In fact, the warrior may enjoy a great cry – a victory cry. By being brave enough to cry, the warrior has broken free of the prison cell and allowed his essence its fullness. "Ahhh, the joy of having room to breathe!" is what the essence will say. Once the warrior has broken free and cried to his heart's content, he will notice that his body is very weak.

You must be very gentle with yourselves at this point, warriors, taking the best care of yourselves until you are healthy and strong. You have spent a big piece of your lifetime pushing yourself down into the prison cell. You have become so good at keeping yourself there that you cannot remember what it is like to have your fullness, or how much energy it takes to keep yourself in the prison. When the energy that was used to keep you there is reconnected to the rest of your body, you will feel extremely tired for a day or so. It is as if you have been carrying around a 100-pound ball and chain. You have developed much strength in your body carrying it the many years you have been living. When you were a child, you struggled with the ball and chain. You had to develop muscles and body shape to help you pull it. You cannot remember how life is without its weight.

What would happen if you cut the ball and chain off, my dear warrior? Would you be able to run faster, leap higher, have more energy for the body, for your purpose? Sure you would. You can use those muscles for the purpose you and the Beginning Without End had planned. I will tell you, my dear warrior, the first thing that will happen is you will feel wonderful in your heart and spirit to be free of that prison. You also will feel tired in your body for a few days. You may say, “Wow, I did not realize that thing was so heavy. I want to rest.”

It is at this time that the warrior starts the journey of self-love and self-care. Love and gentleness are the keys to this part of awakening. When you have found the truth of your essence, you may want to jump for joy or cry soft tears of love for yourself. This is a very necessary process. You can see the truth of the bravery inside you. You can proclaim the warrior’s victory. It becomes time to celebrate your freedom. Imagine someone you love coming home from battle, walking through the door with his tired face proclaiming victory. You will hug him and tell him how you have missed him. You will tell him you are glad he is home and tend to his care. You may cook him a good meal, let him soak in your bathtub, and offer him the comforts of your home. As you would share the graces of your home with your loved one, you can share the same graces with yourself. You will be tired after your battle. It is important to take extra good care of yourself at this time.

This is your first lesson in expressing self-love. It is necessary to commune with your guides and angels who have been protecting you and helping you through these experiences. Although you cannot see us with your naked eye, when you commune with God you can feel our honor, our celebration, our respect for your having gone into battle. This, my dear ones, is the beginning of your connection with your true nature.

After you have recovered from your fatigue, you will feel the alignment take place. Physically you will feel more energized. Emotionally you will feel more tender, and spiritually you will have gained a wisdom. At this point, you will feel the alignment of your body, feelings and spirit. We call this "unifying." It is the transcendence of a belief system into the next phase of your coming home to your essence self. You will begin to feel your connection to the Beginning Without End more strongly.

Now then, dear ones, what about the warrior who has buried himself so deeply that he cannot find himself? This warrior may need to ask for help locating where in the body he is hiding. Maybe he needs to be taught how to feel again or how to feel without being afraid of violence. If the warrior was so abused that he needs help locating himself and healing the dysfunction, he may need to see a good therapist, or healer, or both. Again, this requires bravery.

Some warriors were born with the task of helping other warriors deal with their healing. These healers know what you have gone through and what you are experiencing now and have spent much time learning to heal themselves first.

If you are afraid, listen to that sacred awakening inside yourself. Feel it empower you. Stand tall and take your essence back. Not allowing your warriorship to manifest is a tragedy, dear warrior. Listen to the lie no longer. Swallow the poison no more. You are your antidote.

* * * * *

*The sun started to set and the world became afraid.*
*"Who will help us see in the dark?" cried the people.*
*Truth came out of the night, bright, strong, bold.*
*It illuminated everything and everyone.*
*Its brightness shone with the glow of the stars.*

* * * * *

## LESSON NINE:

# Contacting the Beginning Without End

---

We are the Counsel of Light.

We are so delighted to bring you today's lesson. It is the subject of contacting the Beginning Without End. We will discuss how to find true love, experience true communion in the spirit, have no doubt, and listen with faith and absolute knowing. We will teach you how to move your soul into your very special place of unity and find the warrior within you.

Ask again for your angels, your guides, and the Beginning Without End to be present during the reading. Go deeply into prayer and make intention to feel and find the truth. Ask God to be present with you while you read these words. Ask to feel God's presence and you shall, warrior. Today the lesson is coming from the space of no time, that place where all is happening in the now. Make peace in your heart, dear ones, and allow the love of the Beginning Without End to fill you and lift your soul. Peace be your journey.

I am the Voice.

I welcome you into the journey of self-discovery. Know that I am the voice of the ancients. I am the wisdom of the Earth Mother. I have been here since the dawn of man. I know each and every one of you. I am the way, the truth, and the life, for they are not separate. I am the voice of the mountain, the sound of perfect silence, the inner quest, the voice of desire to connect. I am the space in you that is "the longing," the reason your soul aches at night. I have seen you through all of your lifetimes. I am that which gives you balance. Listen to my words, dear ones. I have been chosen to deliver the message of love.

There is much spiritual seeking in the world today. There are many religions, ceremonies, and blessings to help you connect in the company of the Beginning Without End. Some warriors have felt lost as to which path is the truth. Some warriors cannot move onto a path for fear that they are choosing the wrong path. Some warriors are afraid to find the Beginning Without End because they think they must go through more horrible trials and tribulations to prove themselves worthy. Some warriors are so lost that they think the Beginning Without End does not love them. They feel so bad about themselves that they hide from the Unseen Presence.

The warrior has heard parables about having to make enormous, painful sacrifice to find the Beginning Without End. More pain is something the warrior does not want to experience. The warrior has been told that in order for the Beginning Without End to help him, he must accept one particular faith. Many whom the warrior trusted to help him connect spiritually have been liars, thieves, or cheats, and so the warrior has lost faith in the Beginning Without End. The warrior is told that hell and damnation await him if he does not turn his life to God. He becomes afraid to move on the path because he fears more pain, has feelings of unworthiness, is not willing to sacrifice, and does not want to face the promise of hell, damnation, and the devil. He feels that someone else may get to God, but not him.

How can you, warrior, have fruition in this lifetime without the ability to have communion with the Beginning Without End? You can't, dear one. You must seek inner communion with the Beginning Without End.

If we examine all the issues of fear, sacrifice, unworthiness, hell, damnation, and the devil, we can see that these are just more belief systems keeping you from your true magnificence. These belief systems rob you of your birthright.

They keep you hidden from the world of true glory and don't allow you to have your path. They keep you from communing with the Beginning Without End. They rob you of finding the wonderful state of grace that is just between you and Great Spirit.

We may wonder how great warriors of the past connected to the Unseen Presence. Harriet Tubman could not read the Bible. How did she create so strong a connection to the Unseen Presence? How did she listen to guidance? How did Great Spirit find the way to the native people? They could not read either. They felt Great Spirit's presence and received the teachings anyway. They trusted visions and dreams and prayed, just like Mary and Joseph.

Today we start the lesson of love. We shall talk about the Creator's love, the love that the Beginning Without End has for each and every one of you warriors. Not a day goes by when the Beginning Without End does not think about you. Not an instant goes by when Great Spirit, the Unseen Presence, God, the Creator, the Beginning Without End is not trying to connect with you. The Beginning Without End will impart to you the lesson and levels of love. You see, dear warriors, you have the concept of "love" all bunched up into one small word that is supposed to cover all categories and dimensions. Today we shall enlighten you with the lesson on *love*.

Love has been described as the tender, glowing, warm feelings that you have for something or someone. Love also has different progressions. When we are children, we have love for our caretakers. We love our parents even if they have not taken proper care of us. A grandparent may teach us about love for animals or plants. We may learn to care for a puppy, and in doing so, come to love it very much.

When you get older, love takes on a new dimension when you "fall in love." Suddenly, love takes on a new form. It does not mean that the old love lessons go away – you just progress to a new stage of loving. It is as though you ascend into a new state of being able to love more deeply. It is more intimate and sometimes scary. You have to learn to risk and to take care of yourself and the object of this new kind of love. Love becomes more solid. After time, love has a strength and trust that cannot be measured in the old love way. This new love is deep. You ache for that person with whom you share love. He or she encompasses all your thoughts. You feel as though you cannot love another, and so you both make a commitment in front of God and your family and friends to love each other "til death do you part."

During your time together, love takes on another progression or ascension when the warrior has children. You again find love deepening where your spouse and your child are concerned. The warrior will protect and even lay down her life for the spouse and child. There are not many things the warrior will not do for his or her family.

Love, as we have looked at it here, has different levels. It has a progression or ascension. What is it a progression of? Where does that feeling of love come from? Your love for your parents did not suddenly appear because they took care of your every need. A lot of warriors were abused by their caretakers and still love them.

What, then, is true love? We can say love is a feeling and that is true. Love, however, also is an energy. It is energy just as electricity is energy. It is the force, the glue, the medicine, the body and blood of Christ. Love is food for the body and soul. It is the tone of your planet – the sound that unites the universe. When you fall in love, your appetite changes because you are being fed off your love energy.

Let's make the differentiation here that it is the love within you from which you are being fed. This "food" does not come from the object of your affections. You feel love in your heart. It is your love. The object of your love did not create love in you. You had it there to begin with. If it awakens because another is present, it does not mean they gave the gift of love to you. They can give you the gift of their love, but the energy you feel from being "in love" is your own. It is a common misunderstanding that someone gives your love to you. You feel your love. If someone believes "I would be lost without your love," and the other believes they are giving that love, they are supporting belief systems that are poison and need an antidote. Love is always there inside you and someone can awaken the love in you, but they can't give it to you or take it away from you.

So, if we take the time to look at love in its objective form, we can see that it is an energy that is associated with good feelings, a healthy body, emotions, and spirit. Love energy creates form, substance, and healing. If you further consider love in its objective form, you will learn about and see the power of love energy in the future, because it will help propel you (in physical form) through the air. You see, there are many mysteries still left to help the warrior bring in the age of newness.

You may ask, "How can I utilize love energy? Where does it come from? How do I enhance the love energy in myself for optimum health and life?" We shall explore the answers to all of these questions and more, my dear warrior.

*     *     *     *     *

*Open your eyes, all your eyes.*
*Open your senses, all your senses.*
*Open your heart, all your heart.*
*Quiet your mind, all your mind.*
*All of the answers are there for you.*
*Ahhh, communion!*

*     *     *     *     *

We are the Counsel of Light. We are the Voice, the Knowing, and the Truth. We are pieces of the Beginning Without End. We are whole pieces of the Creator. We have come at this time to awaken all Warriors of Light. The time to unite is at hand. Warriors of Light are pieces of the Beginning Without End – *whole pieces.*

You have heard the term "God is love." It is the truth. God is love. The energy of God or the Beginning Without End is, in fact, love. Love creates form, substance, and healing. Love is an energy. Since the Beginning Without End is the conductor of the orchestra and you are a musician, you can see that you and the Beginning Without End are woven together through love. You become a piece of the orchestra – a whole piece of the orchestra, not a fragment. You play a whole instrument, not just a piece of an instrument.

The point, my dear warrior, is that if God is love and you are a piece of God, you are love also. You are not a fragment of love, but a whole piece of love. This is not something given to you, something shown to you, something learned, or something you look for. It is who you are. In your essence self you are a whole piece of love. That is what weaves you and the conductor together, for you are a whole piece of God.

Do you understand the magnificence of that? It is worth reading again. It truly is the most enlightenment one can have. You are a whole piece of the Beginning Without End. In your objective form you are the force, glue, medicine, tone, and food of God. You are associated with good feelings, optimum health, emotions, and spirit. Through you, the Beginning Without End can create form, substance, and healing. This is why getting to your essence self is of the utmost importance.

The Beginning Without End gives us free will – the option to choose or not to choose. If you choose to find your essence self and manifest your warriorship, as you walk through dissolving your belief systems, you will awaken the essence of the Beginning Without End of which you are a whole piece. From this space you can create unity, at-oneness, abundance, and the age of newness.

Peace, harmony, and love are yours to create, my dear Light Warriors. May you find peace and communion with the Great Spirit.

* * * * *

*I have eagle's wings, Father Sky.*
*I dance in front of the fire of the Earth Mother.*
*I am one with all.*
*I am a piece of everything.*
*I honor it all.*

* * * * *

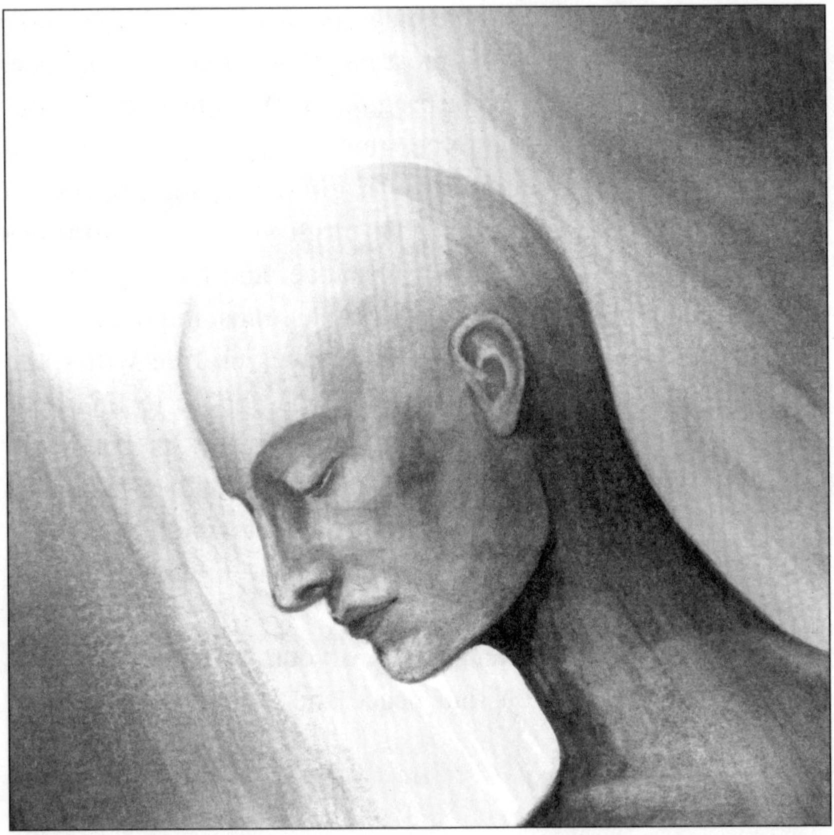

LESSON TEN:

# The Great Awakening

We are the Counsel of Light.

We are very fortunate in our task. We have chosen to help the Beginning Without End awaken those who choose to help bring in the age of newness. It is with much commitment and love that we bring you the next lesson in love. It is within the true essence of love that we honor all those who choose to be Light Warriors. Your love knows not its greatness. You have no memory of your true essence. It is a privilege for the Counsel to have been chosen to deliver to such wonderful beings the message of love from the Beginning Without End.

* * * * *

*It is no longer a task.*
*It is no longer a search.*
*It is the actual state of being.*
*Peace be your journey.*

* * * * *

I am the Truth.

We shall start the next lesson on the subject of love. In our last lesson, we discovered how love was an energy, and that it had a progression into greater and deeper love: love for a puppy, love for parents and grandparents, love for a mate, and love for a child. Since we know we are whole pieces of the Beginning Without End, and the Beginning Without End is love, we too are love. I tell you now, my dear warrior, that learning to use love energy will be the key to your future. This is not just a feeling, it is something that creates. What do you wish to create?

Today we explore the progression and learn about the stages of love. We call the progression of moving through the stages of love "awakening." Since your memory has been erased to bring about the learning of your task, we are simply awakening the memory of your true essence. So, we shall call this lesson the Great Awakening.

When you are a baby, before you learn to talk, you are in your essence. In other words, you are in a state of love. You have fear because you are suddenly without your fullness and have been squished into a tiny body, but you are still love. You remember that you are a whole piece of the Beginning Without End. When the learning begins and the memory starts to erase, the warrior forgets self-love or that she is a piece of the Beginning Without End. The warrior's memory of who she is in her essence is gone, and she cannot remember how to access her wisdom or connection to the Beginning Without End.

The young warrior relies on his caretakers to tell him who he is because he cannot remember. Most of what the warrior learns is his caretakers' belief systems, the confusions that poison the soul. He learns these because his caretakers have not dissolved the belief systems in themselves, either. This then becomes the warrior's job. As the warrior begins the process of dissolving the belief systems (his personal task), he starts to awaken the warrior in himself. He begins to understand that there is a deeper connection to something he can't quite remember.

When the warrior dissolves a belief system, her body, feelings, and spirit align. The warrior experiences a unifying of herself with her purpose. When the warrior is free of the belief system, she experiences a state of grace. The state of grace is a very beloved happening. It is a gift from the Beginning Without End and a celebration of accomplishing a piece of your task. When you attain a state of grace, your essence love awakens. You also obtain a gift from the Beginning Without End.

The Counsel of Light will share these states of grace with you. The warrior can only attain them by receiving them from the Beginning Without End. These gifts are called Sacred Awakenings. They are the most precious gifts that one can receive from the Beginning Without End. They are with you even after you have completed your earthly journey. When you cross over they appear in your energy field as rainbow-colored light. In your world, they would be badges of honor – the kind your soldiers wear for bravery in battle and other heroic deeds. However, these gifts of grace from the Beginning Without End never leave you. You take these gifts with you into your next task. This is how the warrior's soul attains the wisdom of the Unseen Presence. These Sacred Awakenings help the warrior awaken the love energy in the body and energy field – the essence love energy that creates. The awakenings help you find your path and facilitate dissolving your belief systems. Obtaining these gifts also awakens wisdom and compassion in the warrior. It is a very important happening.

I tell you, warriors, these Sacred Awakenings can only be obtained by going within and finding your connection to God. When you think you have found the Beginning Without End, go deeper and find the next awakening. The key is that Great Spirit is without beginning and without end. That is to say, once you start your journey, you will never run out of great awakenings. They are without beginning and without end.

There are seven Sacred Awakenings that are attainable right now. There is an eighth Sacred Awakening; however, it is not its time to be revealed. When the Warrior of the Light attains the age of newness, the eighth awakening will reveal itself. The Counsel does not know when the eighth awakening will be. That can only be revealed by the Beginning Without End.

Remember, these are gifts from the Beginning Without End and can only be given to you by the Creator. No man, woman, lover, preacher, reverend, angel, guide, teacher, or counselor can give you these Sacred Awakenings. It becomes easier for you to attain these states of grace with help from a good facilitator. However, states of grace are from the Beginning Without End only. They are a communion solely between the warrior and the unseen presence of the Great Spirit that is without beginning and without end.

These states of grace, once attained, can be lived in all the time, every day. These are the states of grace your heroes such as Harriet Tubman experienced. She lived in this state of grace all the time – every second of every day. You can see the power of these gifts from the Beginning Without End when you look at the lives of your great heroes. If you can live within these states of grace, you will have found the age of newness. If you are saying to your warrior self, "Harriet Tubman was so great and I'm not as great as she, so I might as well not try," you have lost yourself in a soul poisoning. These gifts from the Beginning Without End are available to all.

It is the Counsel of Light's joyous prayer that the Warrior of the Light finds her chosen path and is able to feel the union of herself and her purpose. We gently ask that you go within and seek the counsel of the Beginning Without End and your guidance, so that you may feel the Unseen Presence. May you find that precious communion between warrior and Creator. May you find fruition in what you seek.

With our undying love,
The Counsel of Light

*    *    *    *    *

*Rest your soul on the promise of*
*the Beginning Without End.*
*Rest your life in the grace of God.*
*Hear Great Spirit speak to you.*
*Feel and hear the Unseen Presence.*
*Dare to walk the path of warriorship.*

*    *    *    *    *

## Lesson Eleven:
# Gifts of the Seven Sacred Awakenings

We are the Counsel of Light.

It is our prayer that all who read these words be blessed by grace from the Beginning Without End. May you find comfort in your soul and take solace in the knowledge that the voice of the Unseen Presence has touched your life, heart, and mind. Peace be your journey as we move to the next lesson.

We will have a brief review of the first Sacred Awakening. The first Sacred Awakening is a state of grace in which the Beginning Without End tells you there is something special and wonderful for you to do in the world. It usually comes in the night when your mind is quiet and you are in deep communion with yourself. This awakening is called Sacred Remembering.

While you are having your remembering, you are in a state of communion with the Beginning Without End. It is purely by the Creator's grace that you are in this state. Many warriors who have just been through a painful learning become quiet in their souls and are able to be in communion. Then when the remembering comes, the warrior believes he is just trying to feel better and shuts the remembering off. And yet before your belief system shuts the Sacred Remembering off, you attain a gift. It is the gift of knowing on a deeper level that you have an incredible purpose. It is the feeling that you are here to save the world. It feels as if you are a superhero. It is true, dear Warriors of Light. You are to change the world forever simply by healing yourself and aligning with the Beginning Without End. The knowledge that comes with this remembering helps you have the will to live through the learning. It gives you a secret strength that is often needed during the time of the learning. It is a very personal and individual gift from the Beginning Without End. This secret strength may be love, tolerance, compassion, tenacity, or wisdom.

It is possible to have more than one of these strengths, but it is true what many of your well-known spiritual texts say, "The greatest of these gifts is love." The love energy creates. The Counsel asks once again, warriors, "What do you wish to create?" Know also, my warrior ones, that the gifts you have earned in previous tasks are still with you in this lifetime.

We believe that the first awakening – Sacred Remembering – is the most important. It is similar to baptism in that a divine authorization between you and the Beginning Without End has taken place. It is a very precious and sweet moment. It is the moment in which you receive your greatest strength. You connect with a deep knowing of your greatness. It is the same special greatness that you feel as you read the Lessons.

The second Sacred Awakening happens when your search for the truth has been fulfilled by finding the truth. Your soul unifies with the Beginning Without End in a spiritual state called Sacred Unification. This connection between you and the Beginning Without End cannot be removed from your awareness. You and the Beginning Without End are joined in a very private, loving union. This is a very personal experience. It is important to know that through this awakening, the Beginning Without End is joined with you on a cognitive level.

This is a time of rejoicing. Your heart becomes full of the love energy that you and the Beginning Without End have awakened. It can be so powerful that tears come to your eyes because you have found your truth. You may feel great excitement, warrior, because you realize this is touching the face of the Unseen Presence within you. It is a most remarkable and memorable state of grace. You will feel the Unseen Presence within your soul.

Sacred Unification creates the gift of faith. It is the kind of faith that can help you dissolve those poisons of the soul. It is the kind of faith through which the warrior absolutely knows without a doubt that the Beginning Without End is with her. During this time the warrior begins to learn how to receive guidance because, for the first time, the warrior has enough faith to receive direction from the Unseen Presence. It is during this time that the warrior's knowledge of a divine path begins to awaken. She begins to realize that the Beginning Without End has a divine transformation for the warrior and the world. This is a time of great change in the warrior. The warrior will experience self-love and a sense of her own dignity. It may be a very private experience, so special that the warrior shares it with no one. She seeks to learn more about her truth and her path. The warrior begins the new learning, the truth learning. She has more compassion for herself and others, and she develops an understanding that all warriors are learning and are healing themselves and the world. She dares to go inside and find the warrior within herself. She dares to manifest her warriorship with dignity and compassion. Many of the warriors reading the lessons are feeling this awakening right now. We honor your space of dignity, dear ones.

At this point, the warrior seeks guidance to help him find his purpose. This is the stage when the warrior will need to find a good healer to help him dissolve his belief systems. The warrior also awakens a very deep love energy for his fellow warriors and the world. The development of love energy awakens the warrior's desire to live and work in his warriorship and to help other warriors bring in the age of the new millennium. While working with a healer or therapist, the warrior starts to complete her personal task. This awakens the Sacred Anointing, which is the third Sacred Awakening.

The Sacred Anointing is the warrior coming into adulthood. This feeling of grace between you and the Beginning Without End has both your personal and world tasks in it. This is when the warrior opens up her instrument case and joins the orchestra. You will start to develop stronger faith and will have the healthy love and desire it takes to accomplish total transformation of your life.

Sacred Anointing is a time of rebirth. It does not always have cheerful feelings. The warrior feels a sense of urgency to accept his task. He feels a responsibility and duty to help the world and others. Sometimes the warrior has to let go of people and ties that are not healthy to his purpose, and the warrior may mourn these lost relationships. Yet the warrior is anchored to his want and wish of being responsible to his purpose. He knows on a cognitive level that he is chosen to help bring in the new millennium. He feels excited and honored to be one of the chosen ones. There is nothing that makes him more happy or fulfilled than to find and carry out his purpose, to join his fellow warriors and have communion. The closeness between the warrior and the Beginning Without End at this point is unbreakable. It cannot be destroyed by anything or anyone.

In this awakening, the gift given to you by the Beginning Without End is that of purpose. The warrior is either a leader, teacher, healer, lover, or intuit. Some warriors who have big tasks have all of these gifts; others have their gifts in different combinations. That is between you and the Beginning Without End. The other gift that you receive at this point is the ability to communicate and get answers from the Beginning Without End. The warrior learns that prayer and meditation are very important at this stage to help her center herself and commune with Great Spirit. The warrior finds that she absolutely needs this every day.

As faith and responsibility to the path unfold, the warrior effortlessly moves into the fourth Sacred Awakening, which is called Sacred Journey. This awakening is the time when the Warrior of Light finds the real sacredness of everything and everyone. This is a time when love energy takes on new meaning, and the warrior is able to find the sacredness in all the chaos. This gift of love heals, creates, glues, and guides the way of the warrior. This is a very sacred gift from the Beginning Without End. Anger gives way to gentleness. Impatience gives way to knowing the natural flow and heartbeat of the Earth Mother. The warrior finds that the world is delightful, that there is magnificence in everything and everyone. The warrior learns to honor all things – animals, the Earth, people, culture, race, ways of worship – all become sacred. We honor all sentient beings. This is a sacred blessing.

From this place, we attain the key to gathering the learning for our path. The warrior knows how to receive the piece of gold that is being taught to him. He shows others how to enjoy the variety in worship, culture, and fellowship. At this point, the love energy in the warrior has grown and emanates so strongly that the warrior becomes a magnet to others who are seeking their paths. The Warrior of Light then can share the warrior ways with others and have fellowship with the new warriors. The warrior now is healing the world just by his presence. The power of the Unseen Presence never leaves him. He emanates the love energy that can only be attained through the grace of the Beginning Without End. You can feel and see this love emanate from the eyes of many great warriors. Look at a picture of Martin Luther King, Black Elk, Princess Diana, Mother Teresa, Jimmy Carter, or Oprah Winfrey. You have many examples of the love energy glowing from within ones who have embarked on the Sacred Journey with the Beginning Without End.

Living within this sacredness opens the way for the fifth Sacred Awakening, which is Sacred Wisdom. This awakening is the gift of your ancestors' wisdom, the sacred wisdom of the ancients. These ancients have the secrets of leading. This is the time when grandfathers and grandmothers impart the wisdom of the unity of everything. This is sacred ground. These wisdoms are not passed to you until your heart can know them as a gift. Your world task comes from this place. It is the wisdom of the Beginning Without End's music that unifies and uplifts the universe. This is the wisdom of Buddha, Jesus, Solomon, Crazy Horse, and Prince Shotoku. These wisdoms are shared with warriors who have attained the gift of the unified mind. This gift from the Beginning Without End comes from journeying on the path of warriorship. This is a very sacred gift. The love energy turns into the power to create and change the world. We cannot fully express the sacredness of this gift of grace. Those of you who have stood in front of the great teachers of today know the sacredness of this wisdom that emanates from them. It radiates from the energy fields of these wise ones. This state of wisdom is the true example of warriorship. It helps the young warrior dream of creating a future. It gives the warrior's soul strength just to be in the presence of these great past and present warriors.

The Counsel of Light wishes to stop the lesson for a moment and honor all those warriors, past and present, whose tireless efforts have helped elevate the universe. We honor the many great warriors who have brought forth the essence of the Beginning Without End. We toast you, and give thanks for your accomplishments, wise ones.

This wisdom creates space for the sixth Sacred Awakening. Sacred Serenity is the grace of the Beginning Without End. From this place of being, the warrior has learned to shut off the thinking process in his head and just be still. The observer does not judge or move. The warrior just is. There are no worries, because you live in the wisdom of the ancients and the Beginning Without End. You know the Beginning Without End will always be there. You speak to him every day. This has often been called "the great apart." In Christian worship, this grace is called "being in the world but not of it." There is a need to be in communion with Great Spirit all the time. Each warrior has his own personal relationship to the Beginning Without End. The warrior is at peace within her soul and is in constant communion. At this awakening, the warrior does not have conclusions about anything, instead, she has at-oneness with everything. There is not a description of Sacred Serenity that is fitting, because to understand this place the warrior needs to experience it. This is quiet wisdom. This is the Sacred Mind. The time of this Sacred Awakening is when enlightenment begins. The warrior knows where to go, who to talk to and what to say.

This place of beingness gives way to the seventh Sacred Awakening, Sacred Unity, which is enlightenment, or Christlikeness. It is knowing that you are not separate from anything. The love energy radiates from you. The warrior knows that he is a piece of the whole. Only now he can hear it, see it, work in it, play in it, taste it, love in it, rejoice in it, and be one with it. You are at unity with all. You understand that there is no separation. You have called all the pieces of the warrior essence back to you. Your life is sacred and you are sacred. This is the sound, tone, creation, form, healing, medicine, and unity of the love energy. This is coming home.

We are the Counsel of Light. There are many more secrets to the wonderful Sacred Awakenings. Each warrior experiences these blessings in an individual manner. These awakenings are just between the warrior and the Beginning Without End. There are many more lessons to teach. Now, however, we end the lesson with love and the intention to bring forth the prayer of dignity of the Warrior of Light.

* * * * *

*The Counsel of Light bows to the warriors of the past.*
*We acknowledge their love, work and commitment.*
*We honor the warriors of the now.*
*We honor the warriors of the future now.*
*You are so dearly loved, warriors.*
*Lead us to the light within.*

* * * * *

## Lesson Twelve:
# Aligning with Your Purpose

We are the Counsel of Light.

We are most excited to help the Warrior of Light align with her purpose. It is such an honor to be in the company of Warriors of Light. It is for the purpose of changing the direction of all humankind, and awakening into unity, that the next lesson is given. This is the lesson of intention from the Counsel of Light. We hope to connect the warrior with the graceful, gentle power of the love energy that creates.

I am the Knowing.

I welcome you to the learning. It is my greatest honor to be with the warrior at this time. If you could feel our excitement on this side of the veil, you would know we are jumping for joy, for that is what the warrior brings to the universe – joy, love, and harmony. You see, warrior, the Counsel is excited to hear the concert of the Earth played by the orchestra of the Warriors of Light. The Counsel is in the audience and is looking forward to the harmony and music created by your unity. The Counsel is excited, because it has front-row seats.

Today, the lesson will start with bringing forth the love energy that creates. We have learned of the Sacred Awakenings. We have learned of intention, belief systems, purpose, and unity. Now, we shall speak to every Warrior of Light. Warrior, we ask you to go within your essence and listen to the voice within you. Call forth the warrior who knows he or she is to help the world awaken. Do not hide that magnificent being. The Counsel of Light wishes to speak to that soldier.

Hello, graceful, gentle one. You have suffered much and we are grateful to you. Go back to the place within you from which you had your Sacred Remembering. Feel this place for a moment. Allow it to encompass all of your being. Ask for help from the Beginning Without End as well as your angels and guides. Ask them to help you *feel* your warriorship. Bring forward your Sacred Remembering, the feeling that you were chosen for something special. Take a moment now and ask for this state of grace from the Beginning Without End to stay with you while you read the lesson.

We fall humble in your presence

When the warrior is developing his warriorship, he is developing compassion, self-love, wisdom, fearlessness, unity and an ability to commune with Great Spirit. The warrior learns that there is a purpose that is his deepest longing, and that by fulfilling this purpose he will have abundance in every part of his life. It is the thing the warrior wishes to do the most. Feel again that Sacred Remembering. Your deepest longing is to help yourself and the world awaken, yet you wonder, "How can I help the world awaken?" You know you could if you knew what it was you were supposed to do. Today we speak to that question. We speak directly to the one who is reading this page. It is no accident that you are reading this.

There are many mysteries, dear warriors, of the new millennium. They are locked inside you – within your essence. In order to unlock these mysteries, you must have intention in walking the warrior path. When you start dissolving the poisons of the soul, you will remember your essence and its purpose. Allow the love energy to move in your soul, warrior one. First, know that dreaming of your future releases the love energy that creates form, substance, healing, and other aspects of yourself of which you may not yet be aware.

Let us together be fearless in looking into the future, dear one. Are you, warrior one, the dear soul who changes the government and helps bring in laws of unity that compassionately govern your planet? Are you, dear one, the warrior who helps the planet unify? Are you the soldier who is the creator of clean energy? Are you, dear one, the creator of new learning for children? Are you, dear warrior, the soul who creates music that heals the body? Are you the healer of violence? Are you the warrior who stops the world from using harmful pesticides? Are you the soldier who ends hunger in your world of new? Are you the preacher, healer or teacher of the new unity? Are you here to join the Hoop Nation into oneness? Are you the teacher of the ceremony of Light Warriors? Are you, dear warrior, the one who discovers new cures for diseases? What is your task?

Each great soul born into the age of Light Warriors has within him or her a very special task and purpose. Feel yours pound in your soul right now. You do not have to know what it is at this moment; you simply need to feel it. You have spent much of your lifetime feeling the poisoning of your soul. Now let your essence feel the antidote. Let yourself feel your power, your love, and your compassion. Allow yourself the privilege of feeling your greatness, your warriorship, your love essence. We are, right now as you read this, releasing your love essence to allow you to feel the love energy that creates.

Again, it is most important that you know that *each warrior of the light has a very special purpose*. It is not just a select few. This is not for the benefit of just a few great people while the rest of the warriors flounder around, aimlessly toiling in pain. This is about creating a new world, and it includes the warrior reading this right now. Are you not curious to know, "What is my gift to the world?" You must ask yourselves,

Warriors of Light, "What is my purpose in being on the planet at this time?" The Counsel says to you right now, warrior, you have a special task that is a blessing from the Beginning Without End. It is your gift to the planet, to humankind, to the universe, to all sentient beings. To bring this gift forward, the warrior must allow herself to feel her empowerment.

Allow yourself to dream right now. Do you want to find your purpose? Do you feel you are here to change the world? Then you must release your essence and take your warriorship. You must stand in the fellowship of the Warriors of Light. Commission yourself to your path. Know that you will have abundance through your gifts and task. Know that everything you need to complete your journey will be provided for you. You can see why the Counsel of Light is jumping for joy. Many warriors are awakening at this moment. Now is the time of the Sacred Awakening of Light Warriors. Gather your brothers and sisters together. Know that those of you with like purposes are soldiers, comrades that have respect for each other. Know that the love for this task is shared by your fellow warriors. You will not envy each other because each one of you has a special gift to bring. Instead, you will marvel at and celebrate each other's individuality. There will be no fighting, because each warrior will be able to receive divine guidance. You will work for the thing that gives you the greatest love and with people who share that love. Reach into your soul and know that you are the pioneers in a new era. Your work is no less significant than that of America's forefathers. Only you are not just creating a new country, you are creating a new world. You, Warriors of Light, are the kings and queens of the new world. Peace be your journey, warrior ones. The angels watch over you.

We shall now move to the lessons of how to awaken the warrior within you, leading you on the road to purpose, abundance, communion, love, and the Beginning Without End.

*     *     *     *     *

*From the mountain tops we shouted,*
*"Ancestors, do you hear my cry?"*
*For I am the warrior you have been waiting for.*
*I am the warrior you have spilled your blood for.*
*I am a whole piece of Great Spirit.*
*I hear your prayers.*
*Empower me with your wisdom.*
*I honor you.*

*     *     *     *     *

LESSON THIRTEEN:

# Dissolving the Planetary Belief in Separation

---

We are the Counsel of Light.

We turn the lesson now to waking the warrior within you. There are many ways to manifest the warrior in you. There are many new things to study and experience in a new and different style of learning. We are very excited to share the awakening lessons. The Counsel of Light wishes to express to you how exciting the time has become. The awakening of Light Warriors has been foretold to us and we have been eagerly awaiting this time. We, the Counsel, feel like young children on your Christ celebration day. There are many presents under our tree. They are the presents of warriors. Every time a warrior awakens, another gift under the tree is revealed. It is a magic time for us. The Beginning Without End has placed a special gift in each warrior. We are privileged to see the gift manifest after the wrapping paper (belief system) is taken off the beautiful present. You have no idea, on your side of the veil, how many presents are under the tree. The Beginning Without End has put them there for all to enjoy.

It is Christmas Eve on this side of the veil. We are also whole pieces of the Beginning Without End and we are waiting for our Christmas Day. On this side of the veil, Christmas Day is called the Sacred Awakening of Light Warriors. Warriors, we honor you and your task, your gifts, your bravery, your love. It is you who grace the Counsel of Light with your presence. Peace be your journey.

I am the Voice.

Today we start the lesson by learning about the belief system that plagues your planet. We call it separation. You believe you are separate from the other side of the veil. When you are born, quite often you are taught that you are born into sin – that you are innately sinful just by your birth. According to many of your spiritual texts, the warrior is never free from sin. It becomes difficult to manifest your warriorship if you are stuck in that vicious cycle.

This belief system truly robs you of your life. Your choices are limited to two. Having ingested this belief system, you will do one of two things, either emanate the poison or try to dissolve it. If you try to dissolve the poison, then you accept that you are sinful and spend your whole life trying to be free of sin, and you never manifest your warriorship. If you choose to emanate this poison, you may not manifest anything. You believe you are doomed from the start, so why even try? You may allow the warrior in you to go to sleep, or you might spend your whole life ignoring the truth.

If you have chosen to try to dissolve the poison, you may seek an "alternative" truth, a truth that you may think you can hide your belief system in. Know that if you choose truth, you can never hide in it. The truth will lead you right back to the place of hiding so you can clear your soul poisons. Each warrior has within him or her this need to find the truth. That is why you found or were given this book to read in the first place.

You have been taught that if you are on our side of the veil, you are "great" or "angelic." Somehow you have learned that the beings on this side are more "worthy" than you are, or that we are closer to the Beginning Without End. On your side of the veil, you have been taught that you were born into sin, that you are worthless, and that you need to repent and find the grace of God. You have been taught that if you don't follow some prescribed set of rules, you may never return to the place from which you originally started, known on your planet as Heaven.

But the truth, dear warrior, is that you were on our side of the veil first. Before you incarnated on the earth, you were on the other side of the veil. You were born of the Beginning Without End first. You were asked by the Beginning Without End to come to this planet, acquire your learning, dissolve the poison of the soul, heal your family lineage, leave the world with a gift, and return home. You were asked to do this and you said "yes." You wanted to help the world awaken. You were chosen by the Beginning Without End to do a specific task because there is no other being that can accomplish this task better than you. The poisons you dissolve will heal your lineage seven generations into the future and seven generations past. You are the best warrior for your purpose. No one is better suited for this task than you are.

You are not "less than" because you are on that side of the veil. You are actually brave, loving, fearless beings underneath your soul poisoning. You are no different than the beings on this side of the veil. The only difference is we have our full essence on this side of the veil. No one has erased our memories. You are equally as wonderful and as important as we are. You have a special purpose. You may marvel at the Counsel's wisdom, but when you are on this side of the veil, you have the same wisdom. The Sacred Awakenings are so the planet can attain the same wisdom on your side of the veil, also. The Sacred Awakenings are so all beings on your planet can awaken into the era of peace and harmony on the physical and spiritual planes, together. This awakening is to help bring in the new millennium. The real secret to the age of newness is to realize there is no veil.

Yours can be a new world. It is as easy to create your new world as it is to destroy it. You have been sent to reclaim the Sacred Path of Warriors. You are not separate from the Beginning Without End. In fact, you are more closely watched and guarded. It is as though you were an astronaut. You have to be an outstanding soldier to be an astronaut. Much training is required to become an astronaut. You send the best men and women into space to bring back knowledge of the universe. You send your most talented people, not your untrained people. When the astronauts are in space, the team at the command center never takes its eyes off them. The astronauts cannot see the command team watching over them, but they have faith that the team members are watching and are at-the-ready 24 hours a day to help with any problem that might occur. There is an understanding between the command center team and the astronauts that the best people have been chosen to work together on the project.

The Counsel of Light is part of the command center team. The astronauts, even though they cannot see the command center, keep in constant communication with the command center team. In other words, the astronauts are in constant communion with the command center team.

Like the command center team, the angels and guides that are on this side of the veil stand ready to help the warrior. We all want to work together with the Warriors of Light. There is not a time when your guides and angels are not ready to help. There is not a time when the Beginning Without End is not trying to reach you. There is not a time when you don't have help ready at your fingertips. The astronaut is never told by the command team, "Now that you're in space, you are not a good astronaut. Because you were thrust into space, you were cast into badness, and that also makes you a bad astronaut. You cannot come home until you are good. If you die before you are good, then you will never return home. If you don't follow these exact rules you may not come home either."

Can you imagine the panic those astronauts would be feeling if they were told something like this? Can you see that if they believed these statements, they would stop work on their true mission and change their goal to "getting back to Earth?" They would do whatever they could to "do the right thing" to get home. They would forget the original reason for their mission. As a result, they would develop all sorts of neurotic behavior. Their fear of being separated from Earth would create fighting among them. They would feel worthless and say, "Oh, why did I accept this mission? How could the command team do this to me? I feel cheated and I'm angry." You can see, warriors, that all sorts of other beliefs, in fact all belief systems, stem from and are created by the thought that you are separate from the Beginning Without End. It is the most devastating of the soul poisonings.

What then is lost is the original purpose of the mission. That sacred knowledge these special people were to bring back to the planet is lost. Their gift to the universe is lost in the lie and confusion of the poison of the soul.

We are the Counsel of Light, the command center for the Warriors of Light. We are at your service 24 hours a day. Know that we are with you even though you cannot see us. Know that you can communicate with us any time, any place.

If you wish to become closer to your purpose, it is good to get some guidance as to what to do next. You do not always have to call your "psychic hotline." You have the ability to awaken your "warrior hotline." It's faster to use and does not cost anything. We shall give you several methods to help you awaken the guidance within you, so you can receive and manifest your warriorship.

But know this, dear one, guidance comes when you truly seek your path. If you wish to manipulate other warriors with guidance for your own gain, it will not manifest. Dissolve the poison and there will be no need for manipulation of any kind.

Before we start the next lesson, the Counsel of Light must again tell you that there is no separation between you and the command center. You are so dearly loved and so closely watched over. You are so precious to the Beginning Without End. It is more than that "God loves you." It is the love energy that created you. You are a whole piece of the Beginning Without End, a brave, loving, fearless, compassionate and wonderful, whole piece of the Beginning Without End. Go within and seek your essence. It does not matter how confused, angry, lost, abusive, or abused you are or have been. There is time to use the love energy to create, heal, glue, and call back the sacred pieces of who you truly are. In doing this, you will find your purpose and help bring in the age of newness – the new millennium. You will help with the most important task ever created – creating a new world. Peace be your journey.

*   *   *   *   *

*A new day awaits us:*
*a new vision,*
*a new clarity,*
*a new walk,*
*a new wisdom.*

*I am the love that creates the new.*
*What shall I create with creation?*
*What is my longing?*
*What is my purpose?*
*I walk toward it;*
*confidence, sacredness, angels, guidance.*
*Peace be my journey.*

*   *   *   *   *

## LESSON FOURTEEN:
# Awakening the Guidance Within You

---

We are the Counsel of Light.

We welcome you to the learning. It is a blessing from the Beginning Without End that we have been chosen for this journey – the awakening of warriors, the awakening of warriorship. If there is but one path that the Counsel of Light had to choose, it would be the path of warriorship that we share with dignity, honor, and love for all Warriors of Light. We now begin the lesson on how to awaken guidance within yourselves, so that you may have communion with the Beginning Without End.

* * * * *

*It is the dance of my ancestors.*
*It is the way of the prophets.*
*It is the silence of the soul.*
*It is the forgotten way of the people.*
*It is time to resurrect the soul of my ancestors.*

*Teach me to walk.*
*Teach me clarity.*
*Teach me contact with myself.*
*I honor those before me,*
*for their wisdoms are unending.*

* * * * *

The Counsel of Light wishes to begin the lesson with several passages from the text you call the Bible:

*Genesis 22:1-2:*

"Some time later, God tested Abraham. He said to him, 'Abraham!'

'Here I am,' Abraham replied.

Then God said, 'Take your son, your only son, Isaac, whom you love, and go to the region of Moriah. Sacrifice him there as a burnt offering on one of the mountains I will tell you about.'"

*Genesis 22:11-12:*

"But the angel of the Lord called out to him from heaven, 'Abraham! Abraham!'

'Here I am,' Abraham replied.

'Do not lay a hand on the boy,' the angel said. 'Do not do anything to him. Now I know that you fear God, because you have not withheld from me your son, your only son.'"

*Matthew 1:20:*

"But after he had considered this, an angel of the Lord appeared to him in a dream and said, 'Joseph, son of David, do not be afraid to take Mary home as your wife, because what is conceived in her is from the Holy Spirit.'"

The Counsel of Light uses passages from this book because it is highly regarded in your culture. There are books written about native people in the United States, such as *Black Elk Speaks*, that also share stories about receiving visions and dreams that gave guidance. Harriet Tubman also received guidance in this way.

Guidance is simply being led by what you call the "Holy Spirit." This spirit is also an energy. It can guide you through your life and purpose. The Holy Spirit is not reserved for Christian religions only. It is Kundalini energy as well. Native Americans call it "Great Spirit." It also has been called the "Unseen Presence." Guidance is not just a feeling. It is also an energy that creates feelings. It is the spirit of the Beginning Without End.

In order for us to learn to receive guidance, we must know two very important things. First, the Beginning Without End wants to talk to us, and secondly, you can talk to the Beginning Without End. You, too, can get answers from the Unseen Presence. It is not just a few prophets and teachers who are able to receive this guidance. You can learn to communicate with the Beginning Without End just as others have.

We first must have faith. That faith will grow into very confident communications. How did Joseph and Abraham learn to speak with angels? Can you imagine if Joseph had woken up the next morning and said, "My, that was a strange dream," and had not paid attention to it? The world may not have received the son of God. The real question in this matter is not why Joseph believed his dream, but rather how Abraham or Joseph, a simple carpenter, learned to speak to angels. How do you learn to communicate with the Unseen Presence so you know where to go and what to do? The parts of the Bible that were written before the Christ child was born and after he died were given to the authors in the form of visions, dreams, and guidance from angels. The prophesies of the Book of Revelation and of Nostradamus were imparted by the "Holy Spirit."

What did these warriors know that the present day warrior does not? They, the warriors of yesterday, understood that the physical realm is not the only reality, and that all "dimensions" are created by the Unseen Presence, including the "dream side." They had knowledge of their purpose. Their sacred remembering was not shoved away, but was instead listened to.

In order to learn to receive "guidance," we must first learn that we are having a conversation from within – from deep inside the warrior's soul. This is a place that does not necessarily have words. Words are not the only form of communication. The warrior also learns that, just as on your side of the veil, you speak and then listen for an answer, or you listen and then speak, you can learn to communicate in this fashion with your guidance. You are developing an intimate relationship between you and the Beginning Without End. The closer you get to your guidance, the more it will help you have your awakenings.

Guidance comes when the warrior has gone within and realizes that she has been chosen for something. Sacred Remembering is a form of guidance from the Beginning Without End. The remembering has no words. If you go back to the first Sacred Remembering you had as a child, you will see that a feeling blossomed inside you and then you put words to the feeling. This one feeling conveyed many sentences regarding what the Beginning Without End was saying to you. One feeling had within it a whole conversation, and without words, you knew it was for you. You could feel this greatness in you, and you knew for a brief second before the soul poison happened exactly what the feeling was saying. You put the words to the feeling.

When the warrior takes responsibility for his purpose and accepts his warriorship, he may start to receive a different sort of guidance. When you make intention to gather guidance for your path, you will have to develop awareness to receive guidance that may come in forms other than feelings. It may be in the words to a song or in some conversation that you overhear in the grocery store. You begin paying closer attention to what is being said to you and around you. When you suddenly hear a song or some other kind of communication, perhaps a conversation, you will know without a doubt that the message is for you. There will be no question that the message is for you. You will hear words, then you will have feelings. The same feelings that created words during your Sacred Remembering create the words now. If the Beginning Without End can communicate with you in this fashion, he will. But know this, dear warrior, the Beginning Without End, your guides, and your angels will communicate with you in whatever way you are best able to receive, whether that is through words, pictures, feelings, or direct knowing.

The next phases of awakening the guidance within you come from the communion of Sacred Journey. This is the catalyst that opens up the next part of the lesson on how to go past basic guidance and receive direction for your purpose and gift. You will have to go within yourself and quiet your mind. Release the chatter within your head. We shall explain different techniques and try to clear any confusion about communicating with the Beginning Without End.

I am the Knowing.

We must know that the closer we get to the Beginning Without End, the easier it will become to obtain guidance. However, we must also know that there are many factors that affect your ability to receive guidance. Some of these factors interfere with the warrior's physical frequencies. Pollutions of any kind interfere with getting guidance. These come in the form of radio waves, microwaves, satellite dishes, air pollution, noise pollution, certain foods eaten, others' negative attitudes, and television. The more "noise" you allow into your life, the more disconnected from your guidance you can become.

It is as if you are at a party and 50 people are having different conversations. You can "tune in" to a conversation across the room, but it is harder than it would be if only one conversation were going on and everyone was listening to the same discussion. You can imagine that, in a room where many people are talking, in order to tune in to one conversation across the room, you would have to really make intention and focus your hearing and vision on that one conversation. The other noise at the party becomes "pollution" and a hindrance to your hearing the important conversation. In such a situation, you would probably have to try a little harder to hear the conversation. It is the same with your guidance. But know this, young warrior, you are in the exact place you are supposed to be to help you connect with your purpose. If you are in the noise of the city, it may be part of your purpose to learn to get guidance there. Maybe you are the teacher of how to receive guidance in the city, despite the noise.

We must tell you of patience and practice. You are learning something new, and the more you practice, the better at it you will become. When you start the process of learning, there will be a period of "detoxing" from old habits, and that will require patience. You have forgotten your essence abilities for quite some time now, and awakening them will not happen overnight. When you walk your path to essence and purpose, getting guidance will become easier for you. The closer to the Beginning Without End you become, the more you practice and make intention, the sooner you will master receiving guidance.

What you feed your body also will influence your ability to receive guidance. When you are in a state of communion, it takes a lot of energy even though you may be just sitting still in peaceful meditation. Your ability to receive guidance will be improved with healthful food. If you eat a well-balanced diet and take necessary supplements, it will help you communicate. Eating well is also a way for the warrior to exhibit self-care. While the warrior is transforming the poisons of the soul and awakening his essence, it is imperative that he take excellent care of himself. Proper rest is also essential. If you are too tired to receive guidance, it will be more difficult.

It is a plague of today's world that warriors do not understand the need for communion, and not just once a week at a church or temple. Harriet Tubman had communion in the forest every day. There is a need to be and feel connected every day. It is breakfast for the soul. If you are overworked, undernourished, and tired, you can expect that connecting to your guidance, path, and purpose will be very difficult. In the cultures of the Earth, working is a plague. It is a disease of the planet. Many of you have learned that working is more important than anything else, and that having a good work ethic is of the utmost importance. The Counsel says that having a "communion ethic" is most important. However, some warriors toil more than half the day, not really knowing why, and for very little return. This leaves the warrior no time for communing with the Beginning Without End, or with his angels, guides, or counsel, which is the very answer to how to stop toiling.

By not having communion between yourself and the Unseen Presence, you are not receiving the messages that will lead you to your purpose. Guidance is of the utmost importance. It will be the way in the age of newness. It will dissolve a lot of stress, fear, and anger if the warrior listens to guidance. It will help you, young warrior, if you practice and have patience. Get proper rest. Eat a well-balanced diet. Lower the amount of noise in your life (quiet the mind). Going for quiet walks as often as you can helps you learn to have communion.

Awareness needs to be developed in order to help you connect to your guidance – awareness of your body, your mind, your thoughts, your feelings and your spirit. These may be things the warrior has been ignoring. People have a tendency to put body, mind, thoughts, and feelings on "automatic pilot." When the warrior's body feels bad – he may notice a cold coming on – he thinks, "I don't want to get sick." But he still goes to work and may take medicine that helps him ignore the message of his body. You have been raised to ignore your body. When the warrior is a young child, he pays attention only to pain and discomfort. If there is no pain, he goes on playing or doing whatever he is doing. You have been taught that your body doesn't have messages for you except to tell you whether you are healthy or not. This is not so. Your body is a big computer full of wonderful information. If you pay attention to it, you can glean its knowledge and its message for your personal purpose.

The warrior also ignores her body when it feels good. If the warrior becomes ill, she knows exactly when it happens. However, she does not pay much attention to when her illness is over. She does not "check in" every morning to see if her body feels good today; she only notices when her body feels aches and pains. In addition, as the warrior gets older, she is taught to ignore pain. It is quite a dilemma in your culture. To go beyond the threshold of physical and emotional pain, especially with males, is perceived as some sign of maturity and bravery. However, this disconnects you from the most fundamental form of guidance.

When you are taught to ignore pain, you dismiss the most basic form of guidance in your life. Pain is used to gauge when you are "overdoing it." When you have overtaxed your body, it would be safe to say that you have overtaxed your spirit as well. Stress in the body from overwork creates stress on the emotions, and it also creates stress in the spiritual realm as a result of not being in or having time for communion. Guidance will force itself upon you in the form of the flu or a cold that keeps you in bed for a few days. This is not the most popular type of communion, is it? When guidance comes as a small illness but you distract yourself with TV, radio, or additional work during your rest, you still cannot receive the message that may be telling you to have faith and seek a new life.

Find your purpose before you drop dead of being overworked. Rest your body, feelings, and spirit in communion with the Beginning Without End. If you are living and working within your purpose, that is communion. It gives you the most happiness and fulfillment in your life. It creates optimum health.

If the warrior develops awareness of her body, feelings, and spiritual self, she then will be able to have balance between her purpose and her duties until her world task manifests. You can have optimum health and happiness while you manifest your purpose, especially if you receive the guidance and have the communion you need every day. These things are as essential as food and water. You have three separate areas in your life that need nourishment: your body, your feelings, and your spirit. The body needs good nutrition and exercise. The feelings need self-love, deep contact with another, and uplifting feelings. The spirit needs communion with the Beginning Without End, angels, and guides. These essential elements create an optimum life. All of these areas of your life need the love energies of yourself and the Beginning Without End.

For you to begin learning guidance, we will first teach you a morning exercise that is not physical. We call it "check in." When the warrior first gets up in the morning, he will do his morning caretaking, and before he leaves his home and starts his day, he will check in. First, he will ask his body, "Body, how do you feel?" Then the warrior will wait for his body to tell him how it feels. The body may say: "I'm hungry"; "I'm tired"; "I'm sore"; "I'm in good shape"; "I feel no pain"; "My back hurts"; "I need more rest"; or "I feel swollen." Whatever the body is saying, the warrior will make note of. The warrior does not have to do anything but listen. We are learning to let the body talk, and teaching the warrior to listen. If the warrior wishes to do something, like give the body food, then he may after he finishes checking in.

Second, we shall check in with the feelings. What do the feelings say today? Maybe they say: "I'm happy"; "I'm stressed"; "I'm angry"; or "I'm sad." Whatever the emotions say, with this exercise, we don't try to change that. We just try to listen to what our emotions are saying.

Third, we check in with the spirit. What does your spirit say today? Are you feeling connected to the Beginning Without End or not? Do you need time for communion? Are you needing meditation, prayer, or a quiet walk by yourself? Do you feel your purpose this morning?

We check in every morning for several days until we automatically do it every day. Not only does this exercise develop self-care, more importantly, it develops awareness. You will need to develop awareness in your world in order to receive messages from your guidance. Guidance can come in the form of body sensations, emotions, or messages from spirit guides. But before the warrior can learn how to be in touch with these things, she must first know how to be in touch with herself and how she feels normally.

After you feel comfortable checking in with yourself, we will add checking in with your workplace. You will ask yourself, "What does the atmosphere at my job feel like today?" Then listen for an answer. We can learn to feel whether people are happy, stressed, or tired. We do not have to join them in their unhappiness or happiness. We are just trying to listen to and feel what is happening in the workplace. We are making note of how other people are moving around in their work environment. You should make note of the interaction between yourself and others. Once you have noted the differences between yourself and your co-workers, you will find that people who are not aware are easily influenced by the general workplace atmosphere. You, on the other hand, are observing the actions of others and then observing your own actions. We don't judge, we just observe the difference between ourselves and others. What does your body say? What do your feelings say? What does your warrior spirit say?

Next, we shall ask you to limit the amount of TV you watch and movies you rent or see at the theater. If you can totally turn these things off for a while, that would be ideal. It would be most beneficial if you could do without these distractions for four to six months. It is stressful on the body to go through the emotional ups and downs experienced by watching many movies and TV shows. It is hard on the emotions and spirit as well. They are part of the pollution we are trying to limit so you can quiet your mind enough to receive guidance.

You will go through a detoxification period when you eliminate TV and movies. You are learning to be in your center. You are feeling your body, emotions, and spirit. It will help if you have alternative things to do that will keep you in your young warriorship. Listen to spiritual music. Have a prayer circle. Feast with warrior friends. Read a spiritual book. These are things that will help you have communion, quiet your mind, and change your life with the intention of finding your essence and purpose. This is about the awakening of you, the start of a new and exciting journey.

Peace be your journey, young, precious warrior. We view your birth into your purpose the same way a proud parent sees the birth of his or her precious child. It is the birth of your warriorship. Happy Birthday, magnificent soul.

*  *  *  *  *

*It came as no surprise as we looked at the sky . . .*
*another day the Creator had made a beautiful sunrise.*
*No sunrise is exactly the same:*
*each is individual, unique, just as snowflakes and trees.*
*It is the magnificence of creation,*
*the flow of the Almighty.*

*The Earth shall watch*
*and the sky shall witness creation.*
*No two sons rising are the same.*
*It is harmony.*

*  *  *  *  *

## LESSON FIFTEEN:
# Planetary Interconnectedness

We are the Counsel of Light.

It is our purpose to help the planet awaken into the age of newness. It is our task to send you the teachings that you now are experiencing. It is your purpose to tell as many of your fellow beings as possible this message. We impart that knowledge to you now. It is with our sincerest love and devotion that we, the Counsel, undertake this task. You are honored and loved. You are magnificent beings of light, wisdom, and love. Find that within you and manifest your purpose. The time for awakening is now. Peace be your journey, dear ones. We watch over you.

I am the Voice.

I honor all those beings that have come to the place of learning and remembering. You have forgotten who you are and your purpose. You have forgotten how sacred you are, how sacred everything is and how it is all intertwined. You have forgotten the weaving of the universe from the hand of the Beginning Without End. All things come from the Beginning Without End. All is sacred. You are sacred. You are a piece of the Beginning Without End. A whole piece, not a fragment. All things are sacred and when in balance have unity, peace, love, and abundance. You are all woven together and no one thing can live without the other. All parts are necessary to create the whole.

You have not remembered the early lessons of the ancients, grandfathers, and grandmothers. When you lose connection to the Earth, you don't remember the simple sacredness of the everyday.

To help you remember this sacredness, the Counsel of Light will remind you that if there is no air, *everything on the planet dies*. If there is no water, *everything dies*. If there is no heat, *everything on the planet dies*. If there is no cold, *everything on the planet dies*. Not just a species, but everything. So you beings on this planet are as well an endangered species, because without you, *everything on the planet dies*. Without plants, *everything on the planet dies*. Without animals of all kinds, *everything on the planet dies*. You all need each other. You are all connected. One is not more important than the other.

It is true that the lesson the Voice is now sharing with you is basic. It is in the basics that you are most out of balance. Many beings on this planet feel that because there are so many of you, you are not an endangered species. Many of the beings on this planet feel as though there is someone else chosen to bring balance and carry these changes out. If that is true within your being, why are *you* here, dear one? Do you feel that you have been sent down here to toil in pain and suffering? If you believe that, do you think the animals are sent down here to toil in suffering? Are plants sent down here to toil in suffering? What is it exactly that you believe? Do you wait for another chosen one to tell you what you believe? Why are certain people chosen and you think you are not?

I tell you, dear one, that you are a great warrior, as is everyone and everything. The human beings on this planet have forgotten that the whole planet is the Garden of Eden. The garden is not just a place on the planet, but the whole planet. Within the Garden of Eden are the voices of the mountains, the water, the animals, and the trees. Each speaks its wisdom of the Creator's love. Within the Garden of Eden, among the animals, there are the two-leggeds. Within each two-legged is the wisdom of the Creator's love. Within you there is a special message to the world. Go within. Find your message and help your soul and the world awaken into the age of newness. It is as if you are putting a puzzle together. Every piece is needed. There is no piece that is greater or lesser. *Every piece is needed to create.* Yours is needed as much as the birds' or fishes' pieces are needed. *You cannot fully see the sacredness of all things until you fully and completely feel your very own sacredness.*

The Counsel of Light cannot convey how sacred each piece of the Creator is. If you had the Beginning Without End's shoes, would you not think, "How special that I have his shoes"? If you saw the Beginning Without End and he gave you his robe, wouldn't you feel thankful, special, and loved? Be of good cheer, warrior ones. You are his children, the heirs to the throne. Whatever you wish to create with the love energy that you are, the Creator wants to help you create. It is a pure expression of the Creator's love for you when he creates through you.

Peace be your journey, dear warrior one. For at the warriors' gathering, the kingdom of Heaven lies within the heart of the warrior. Within that heart is the gift of transforming the Earth into a heaven. Yes, it is so. This is the time of transition. Come join the celebration of awakening. Create the feast of the new. Feast at the table of the new. Feel the sacredness of the new. Show your very sacred newness and let the world rejoice. It is we who bow at your feet, magnificent being of light.

* * * * *

*Feel my presence in every cell of your body,*
*for I am the Creator.*

*Feel my love in every beat of your heart,*
*for I am the Creator.*

*Feel my love in every breath you take,*
*for I am the Creator.*

*Feel my presence in every flower you smell,*
*for I am the Creator.*

*Feel your creation,*
*for I am the Creator.*

* * * * *

## Lesson Sixteen:
# The Great Mother Earth

Welcome to the learning, warrior one.

We are the Counsel of Light.

It is an honor to be in service to the Beginning Without End. Today we bring joyous news of purpose and light. The Counsel of Light shall be speaking of the transition of the planet. This becomes a two-part lesson we speak of today.

First, we shall learn of the planet from the view of the groups of people living on the planet at this time. It is a very common practice in the culture of now to divide the planet into sections and then name them. Some of the sections are fought for with bloodshed. This bloodshed shows the world that this section belongs to a certain group. Some of these groups have different names, such as China, Turkey, England, America, and Africa. From this view, the warrior can see that he belongs to a group. He feels he must defend his group and protect it from harm. He must help his warrior children grow and flourish within the land that he defends with his life.

The group of people that lives on a section becomes very proud of the section it defends. The groups name these sections with much pride and deep love for them. Some names are for deserts, mountains, lakes, oceans, and forests. The section of the planet becomes even more defined with more names: the Gobi Desert, the Rocky Mountains, Mount Fuji, the Pacific and Atlantic oceans, Ayer's Rock, Mount Everest, Mount Shasta, Mount Saint Helens, and the River Thames. The group claims and shows ownership of its section. Using names in their section helps the group members with directions, and agreement lessens confusion that would be caused if they did not agree on the name.

However, this also gives the idea of ownership of the section to members of the group. It is their section and they can do what they want with it. They try to improve the section for the group. They clear trees and plants out of the way to build homes. They dam up water supplies to run through pipes to their homes and to water the crops that feed the group. They try to improve the health and way of living of the group and its children, keeping them strong and vigorous in case they must fight later to defend their section of the planet.

This is a noble act of true love and is not meant to harm anyone. However, it hides the truth of what this planet is. This way of life cuts you off from having to speak with the planet. It can allow you to go to sleep and let someone else take care of the decisions of the planet. Sleeping in this manner cuts you off from your purpose. The warrior becomes unaware that he can talk with the planet and ask for help, guidance, balance, and abundance. The warrior becomes unaware that the planet is a living being. The planet becomes near crisis in its ability to help the group if no one in the group is willing to listen. It becomes even more critical when the group does not know that the planet can speak, that it has its way of communicating with the group, and that the planet knows everything. This planet has been here since the beginning of time; it knows every time you have been born onto it, and every place you have lived. The planet knows your purpose. The planet has kept track of every era in which you have lived, died, and been reborn.

The Counsel of Light wishes to call the planet by the name the native people gave it. The word "planet" can create the sense of an inanimate object rather than recognising the beautiful, living being that she is. So to give her the proper, truthful definition, we shall call her the Great Mother. For the Great Mother is the carrier of all life. Within her she carries the wisdom of all. We shall try to impart the greatness of the Mother to you now, so that you may learn to feel her.

In the Bible, the Great Mother was the Garden of Eden. But the whole planet is the Garden of Eden, not just one place on the planet. The Great Mother does not look like the moon, with only a section of it being the Garden of Eden. It is the entire being of the Earth that is the Garden of Eden. The Great Mother gives birth to all life upon her – animals, people, fish, and plants – and has deep love for her children, the way a warrior mother loves her children. That is the Great Mother.

The Great Mother is a divine piece of the Creator, the One who is Without Beginning and Without End, with whom all things are possible. The Great Mother has the divine love of the Creator within her. This love is the heartbeat of the Great Mother. She knows each and every warrior on the planet. You are her beautiful, precious children. She is the Great Mother and she knows the lives of each of her children, your pain, joy, confusion, love, and anger. It is no different for the Great Mother than it is for the warrior mother. The warrior mother who has children knows that each child is different and brings something special to the warrior family. It may be that the child loves music, art, science, cooking, or humor. The warrior mother knows that each child will bring a special gift into the family and then into the world. The mother loves each child's special gifts. Each is a beautiful being of love and light.

When the child needs to be fed, loved, advised, comforted, or guided, he goes to the father and mother and speaks of his need so he can be cared for. Most of the time the father and mother know of the child's needs before the child knows.

The father is the Beginning Without End. The mother is the Earth, the Great Mother, the Garden of Eden. You may talk with them and receive guidance, comfort, love, and communion. When the warrior speaks with the mountain, she is speaking to the Mother. Even if the mountain has "male energy," it is still the Mother. It is similar to when a warrior child walks up to the mother's elbow and begins speaking to the elbow. The warrior child is still talking to the mother. It would be the same if the warrior child spoke to the knee, the heart, the back, or the ribs. It matters not where the warrior child speaks; she is still speaking to the mother. No matter where the child is, the mother can always hear the child speak. If you speak to the river, the forest, the mountain, or the ocean, it matters not, for you are still speaking to the Great Mother.

It is important at this time to note that the Mother has many different energies. The warrior who goes to the ocean feels the ocean's energy. The warrior who goes to the mountain feels the energy of the mountain. If the warrior is awakened, she will notice that the mountain has a different energy than the ocean. It also has a different energy than the desert. All of the energy of the universe is within the Great Mother. These energies help keep the warrior healthy and feed the energy field around the physical body of the warrior.

We can explain these energies as the umbilical cord that feeds the child within the womb of the warrior mother. Even though you cannot see the energy with your naked eye, it still exists just as electricity does. It nurtures and cleanses the energetic field, or the aura, around the body. This cleansing is similar to when a lioness cleans her young cub. The lioness uses her tongue to clean the body of the cub. It is the same with the universal energy of the Great Mother. The Great Mother has what is termed by your culture as both male and female energy; yin and yang Chi or Qi energy. All are from the Great Mother. When the warrior sees the true nature of the Great Mother, he can see why she is in such distress.

The Great Mother will then intervene in the affairs of her confused children and lovingly show them that they are interconnected and that one is not greater than the other. She will teach them love and help transform them into peaceful, loving Warriors of Light, showing them how to appreciate each other instead of warring against each other and hurting the Great Mother in the process.

Teaching the children to transform their confusion into wisdom brings the Counsel of Light to the next lesson of warriorship. It is with great dignity and reverence for the Beginning Without End that we end the lesson of the Great Mother and move to the transition of the Great Mother.

*   *   *   *   *

*I sleep in the cradled arms of the Mother.*
*I am fed by the light from her soul.*
*I am a child of the Creator placed in the Mother's arms.*
*Blessed am I among souls.*
*I walk in the light of the Mother and Father.*

*   *   *   *   *

LESSON SEVENTEEN:

# The Transition to a New Age

We are the Counsel of Light.

We welcome you to the learning. We continue the lesson of the transition of the Great Mother. It is with great honor that we bow to those who have chosen to be here at this time. You cannot remember who you are. You are so loved and cared for. We thank you and celebrate your task. You are the bringers of the now, and this is no small task. Blessings be bestowed upon you for your wonderful love and kindness, for this is the path of warriors.

Today we speak of transition and transformation. First, we shall speak of transition. Transition is the passing from one phase or state to another, the "changing over to." It is part of your task as a warrior, to help the Great Mother change over to the age of newness. This is not as easy as it sounds. It is as great a transition as was moving into the Industrial Revolution.

We shall use this as the example. The first stage of the industrial age was to create things that were not on the Great Mother at that time. Some warriors had to go within themselves and create when the rest of the world thought they were out of their minds. Some of these inventions were the cotton gin, the automobile and, of course, the airplane. The men who invented these machines are now heroes of your world. They are said to be leaders and inventors, men of daring. The important thing that must be learned here is that these warriors created something that did not yet exist on the Great Mother. The creation came from within each warrior. This was their Sacred Remembering, because what they created was not yet on the planet. They were born with their task, just as you were.

The second phase of the Industrial Revolution was bringing the invention into the world and showing how it worked and how it could improve people's lives. However, these inventions did not improve the lives of everyone overnight. Some people lost their jobs and were replaced by new machines. This caused fear and anger until a new skill had been learned. Many people were frightened of the new and wanted the old way back. Some could not afford to take advantage of the new developments for quite some time. This was the transition phase. This phase takes time. There were those who were resistant to change and who found it very difficult to move into the industrial age.

The most important point about this period in time is that the change came whether the warrior wanted it to or not. Some were the inventors, some were the buyers, some were laborers, but all had a part. It came no matter what the argument. It was the awakening of that period in time.

That time has long passed, and the warrior is now moving from the age of technology into another age of newness. This time is also new on the Great Mother. The tasks are within you. This age of newness comes with bringing in the new and undergoing a metamorphosis into remembering of spirit and closeness with the Beginning Without End.

You must seek the help of the Creator if you want to manifest your purpose. It has always been that way and shall always be that way. You cannot create without Creator. Creation is a gift from the Beginning Without End. Your purpose does not come knocking at your door. It will not be hand-delivered to you. You must seek your purpose within yourself. You must go within and bring forth that which is you and the Creator. This phase helps the young warrior develop into an adult warrior. It is the most important part of the learning because it becomes the awakening phase of the warrior's development.

The next part of the warrior's transition is harmony. After you have made the transition to newness and have balance, there will also be harmony.

This is the spiritual revolution. It will have the same qualities as the industrial revolution. First, there will be the creation and invention of things that may not be on the Great Mother yet. Second, the changes are coming whether you accept your task in them or not. This may cause fear in some warriors and not in others. Third, after the transformation, there will be peace, love, and unity. There will be balance between you, the Beginning Without End, and the Great Mother. Finally, remember that this is awakening, not punishment. Know that the more warriors that awaken and manifest their purpose, the easier the changes will be.

Since this is the spiritual revolution, how we relate to the Great Mother is one of the biggest changes we will experience. She is trying to awaken her sleeping children and have them honor her and her power. There is nothing created by man that the Mother cannot easily destroy. She is tearing down your cities and your inventions of old to help you awaken into the age of newness. Your ways of old are being challenged to facilitate your awakening.

One of the biggest "drug" problems you have in your world of old is money. It is more addictive than cocaine, heroine, cigarettes or alcohol. You will sell your soul to work for someone who gives you money. You will stop finding the purpose that is within you for someone to give you a minimum wage. You cannot have abundance doing someone else's dream, purpose, or task. People will kill one another for the money drug. They rob, steal, and become very afraid if they don't have the money drug. With this much fear, how can anyone find their purpose?

The Great Mother is going to break up your money habits. You will then have to seek the counsel of the Father and the Great Mother for guidance. It is easier if you seek their counsel now versus even a year from now. To hear the Great Mother, you must shut off your radios and TVs. Become quiet in your mind and go outside to be with the Great Mother. Ask your counsel of guides and angels to help you. Go for a picnic with the Father and the Great Mother. Let her rock you in her arms. These changes come with a lot of fear. People are very dependent on the technology of today and have forgotten the Great Mother. She is speaking to all the warriors. Pray together and create the community of the new. This, my dear warrior, is the age of newness. It is as easy to create a new world as it is to destroy yourselves.

Let us end by giving you a hint. The Father and the Great Mother will not let the children destroy them. It is as it should be. Peace be your journey, dear ones.

## Lesson Eighteen:
# The Five Stages of Healing

---

We are the Counsel of Light.

We welcome all those who wish to gather at the table of warriors and accept their purpose. You have learned much by listening to the Counsel explain the task of the warrior, the task of the Counsel, and the Beginning Without End. It is your choice to join in the healing of yourself and the awakening of the Great Mother. If you choose to participate, you must learn the five stages of healing.

The first stage is feeling so horrible about yourself that you try to hide from the world in many clever disguises. The second stage is acceptance that these disguises or masks are not who you truly are. The third stage is discovering who you are and examining how and why you took on your disguises. There is much anger and blame at this stage. This is the place where most warriors get lost. They forget that they are the healers and that they are responsible for each and every detail of their lives that is amiss. It is as if you got the flu from your parents. You are angry that you have the flu. You ask "How could you do this to me? My body is sick because of you."

Dear warriors, even if you did get the illness from your parents, you now have to be responsible for your health. If you are not well, it is your own doing and no one else's. No one can heal the illness in your body but you. You can make yourself even more sick with your own anger by saying: "If you had not made me sick with your flu, then I would not be angry and more sick. Thus, my anger is your fault, too." Again, it matters not where the flu came from. Your anger is yours and no one else's. Only you can heal the body and the anger, or it will progress into a greater illness.

The fourth stage of healing is the acceptance that you are the only one who can heal your flu. There are many different forms of the flu, but you must heal only your flu, for it is the only one you can heal. By healing your flu, you heal it in the rest of your lineage, seven generations forward and seven generations back.

The fifth stage of healing is the awakening process. Now is the time to learn of the great warrior within and align with the Beginning Without End. This stage awakens guidance, peace, compassion, love, and purpose. At this stage of healing, the warrior begins helping others heal by using the gift that aligning with the Beginning Without End has awakened.

It is the same with the Great Mother. You are in the third stage of healing with respect to the Great Mother. You may blame each other for causing the state that you are experiencing now, but it does not matter. Acceptance of the state you're in is part of the warrior's path. Do not blame what your forefathers did. Your forefathers helped the world evolve into a new age that was not yet on the planet. It is again time to awaken and create something new that is not yet on the planet. You were chosen because there are no other warriors on the planet at this time who can better do the purpose that is within each of you.

You are the heroes of tomorrow. You are the transition team. You are magnificent beings of light. You must own this in order to help yourselves and help the Great Mother. It has been done many times in history before. Listen to the great words of your heroes and know that you are in their company.

You were not chosen for your inability but rather for your ability. If you cannot find it, and need help from a healer, there are many great healers on the planet today to help you heal yourself. Many know of this great purpose already and can help you find your purpose. At the end of this book, we shall give resources to help the warrior find assistance in awakening and in the healing he or she may need.

Find or create a Warriors of Light group within your neighborhood so you can feel companionship with fellow warriors. Feast together and pray together. Follow the sacred walk of warriors. Meditate and be with the Beginning Without End. Find other reading material to help you find your purpose. Most importantly, you must look within and find your special path with the Creator. Once you have healed yourself, awakened the warrior within you, and proclaimed that you wish to help heal, know that what you are to help heal in others is already within you.

* * * * *

*I have walked the road.*
*I have tasted every step of the path.*
*I am looking at the outcome unfolding.*
*Peace, love, abundance,*
*and the dance of warriors.*
*Rejoice.*

* * * * *

* * * * *

*From the sacred place within,*
*from the divine within,*
*to bring it without,*
*and within,*
*with another*
*is the experience*
*of touching the face of Creator.*

* * * * *

## Lesson Nineteen:
# Relationships

We are the Counsel of Light.

We welcome you to the learning. This is a glorious time in history and we are excited to be a part of it. We give thanks and honor to those who have worked so hard. We honor those who were before us that gave their love to the Great Mother so that this great awakening of the soul could manifest. Peace be the journey in the universe.

Today we speak of relationships between warriors. There could be a whole book of lessons written solely on relationships. The Counsel of Light wishes to give you clues about relationships and contact with another person. You can then explore other written material on the subject of relationships. In order for you to fully grasp this awakening, we shall speak of it in three parts: love relationships with the self, love relationships between partners, and love relationships with family. We shall start with a brief review.

Love is the energy of the Beginning Without End. In its objective form, it is associated with positive feelings or emotions and a healthy body and spirit. Love creates form, substance, and healing. It is the creative force within you. It is the sound and tone that unites the planet. The Beginning Without End is love. You are a whole piece of the Beginning Without End, and therefore you are also a whole piece of love. You are an energy that can create, heal, and have form and substance. This is a very powerful gift from the Beginning Without End. There is not a better energy for healing.

To unleash the love energy within you, first you must use it with yourself. That is to say, warrior one, that using the love energy to heal yourself, love yourself, and create for yourself is your first journey. By doing this, dear one, you strengthen your connection to the Creator. You have your Sacred Awakenings and can form the needed alliances between your guides, angels, and the Beginning Without End. The love energy helps you align yourself to the wonderful, beautiful purpose that the Creator has just for you. Your purpose will give you the most happiness and abundance. The Beginning Without End wants to show you how to use the love energy to manifest whatever is your creation, your deepest longing.

Here is a clue, warrior one. Your purpose is that which gives you the most happiness. This is not to be confused with that which gives someone else the most happiness. This is just for you personally. If you help another warrior reach her purpose and do not know what yours is, that is not having your own purpose. Helping other warriors achieve their purpose is a wonderful hiding place for the warrior who is afraid to manifest her personal path. A warrior who will not go within out of fear is clearly indicating a soul poison that is hidden within. We are not saying that it is not good to help another warrior achieve her purpose. We are saying that not to achieve yours is a tragedy, warrior one. Prayer, meditation, and loving healing are needed for that magnificent being to help manifest her purpose.

The warriors on the Great Mother at this time have just barely scratched the surface regarding the use of the love energy. Many books are now being written on the subject of loving and healing the self. Spend some time reading other materials that can help. Learning to use the love energy on the self will require help from a good healer and facilitator. This is a process that is happening now all over the Great Mother. There are many great healers on the Great Mother at this time.

When using the love energy for yourself first, a metamorphosis of the soul starts to take place. Suddenly people and the world will treat you differently. The energy field around your body will emanate the love energy out to others and to the world, thus creating healing for the planet. Most importantly, dear warrior ones, since we are all interconnected, the healing you do for yourself helps heal everyone. It is a holographic universe. So helping yourself is the most important thing you can do for yourself and the world. This form of awakening has a trickle-down effect. It will trickle to your loved ones, children, family, and people you would never expect it would change or help.

You must know that all the answers are within you. This statement shall be explained in two ways. The first involves the concept of self-responsibility. You are the creator of all your actions and reactions. You must therefore look within yourself to find the reasons why you have created what you have in your life. For example, you may have discovered a soul poison within yourself and spent much of your life reacting a certain way to dissolve or emanate the poison. Using the love energy to gently and lovingly find the antidote for that poison will, for the first time, open up the truth and let the love energy in. At that point you can have a warrior's action instead of a poisoned reaction. This is the key to working with the love energy. It is also part of your learning to use the love energy to help you create form and substance and purpose. Later, as your self-awakening process opens more, you will be able to access your love energy all the time, without the struggle of the first learning. This is also how the soul awakens into the age of newness. This is the great awakening of the soul. This is the great change on the Great Mother at this time. She has many helpers assisting her with the awakening of her children.

The next part of using the love energy with the self is learning to use it to create that which you love. It is to go deep within the self and manifest that which you love the most. It can be art, science, dance, poetry, gardening, or maybe something that is not yet created on the Great Mother. You see, dear one, it is only when you go deep within the self that you find you have had your love energy within you always.

This takes us to the next lesson of the love energy: love relationships between partners. Because you are a piece of the Beginning Without End, which is love, you are love also. You were love energy at birth. You soon forgot this, but slowly and with time, the love energy began to re-awaken. You are now awakening the love energy that is already within you. It is yours.

It is very important for the warrior to know that the love energy within the self was there at birth. We are just re-awakening the love energy that already is within you. The Counsel of Light cannot express how important this is. It is your essence that we are awakening – the whole piece of the Creator that you are. Every piece of the Creator is sacred. You are sacred. Every last piece of the Creator is needed to create the whole. Every piece of Creation is the love energy. You must awaken your piece of that love energy. When you do, you have helped heal yourself, the world, and the universe. You become the musician in the orchestra conducted by the Beginning Without End. You bring balance to the Great Mother and help the planet awaken. Not a bad accomplishment for just healing yourself, warrior one! The most wonderful piece of awakening the love energy is how deep the relationship between you and the Beginning Without End becomes. It is unbreakable, without separation.

"What then," you may ask, "happens when you meet another warrior on the Great Mother and a lot of love suddenly awakens within you?" You warriors now call it "falling in love." For the purpose of this lesson, we shall change the name to "awakening in love." For that is another form of awakening the love that already exists within the self. Love has many forms in relationship; however, awakening in love is the closest to divine love there can be. It is a glimpse of the love that is from the Beginning Without End. When you meet someone and both of you have awakened the love energy, the first thing that happens is the Sacred Remembering. The feeling of some deep destiny between the two of you awakens. It awakens silently in each person. You may not discuss it, but if you spoke to one another regarding Sacred Remembering, you would find that you both have a deep feeling of something big and really important that you are to do together. There also would be the feeling of not yet knowing what it is, which is also true.

Awakening in love is a clue to having purpose with someone. It also is the process of helping each other dissolve the poisons of the soul. Again, the process of awakening the essence self is an individual process, yet the purpose may and can be together with another warrior. Maybe the two are teachers of love and relationship in the age of newness.

When awakening in love occurs, it is important for each warrior to speak with his or her partner in order to help each other awaken the truth. You may be introducing your partner to warriorship. If you have a partner now, speak with him or her and see if that same feeling of Sacred Remembering is in his or her soul also. If the two of you agree, then it is time to go within and manifest the creation that is locked within both of you. You may seek out a healer or facilitator to help you find what it is the two of you are to do. Meditate and pray together to help find the piece that each of you is to contribute. Know that Warriors of Light walk the path of unity and oneness. They are dedicated to the awakening of themselves, the Great Mother, and closeness to the Beginning Without End. The path the warrior walks is *without beginning and without end.* This is important to help keep a relationship deepening into warriorship. Once the partners have found their purpose and are working in it, they must go deep within and find the next awakening, working together to awaken together. Know that the love between you is a gift to the Great Mother and helps heal her. It also helps create the community of the new, which is a later lesson. For now, let us explore one more lesson on the love energy.

We shall briefly speak about the third facet of love relationships: how using the love energy to heal the self also heals the family. When you heal yourself, you unblock energy that is stuck in your energy field. This unblocking can be felt by other members of the family. Suddenly you may hear others comment about how cheerful you have become. Maybe they have noticed that you have a glow around you, as though you have awakened in love. But most important is that you will have developed a deep compassion for where they are in their process. You may see them from a different view. You may see their pains of soul poisoning, but instead of harboring anger, you can just allow them the space to be as they are.

Understanding this creates peace within you. If they go into their soul poison and say something hurtful to you, you will realize that it is their soul poison speaking. You will know that they are responsible for the action or reaction they have, and that it has nothing to do with you. You can just stand in your warriorship and quietly ask for the love energy to fill you. Just your presence will start the change process.

We honor the task ahead. Know that you are loved and cared for by all who work in service to the Beginning Without End. Know also that you are a magnificent being of light, full of the love energy. Peace be your journey, dear one.

* * * * *

*Passion is creation from the love energy of the soul.*
*What do you wish to create, dear one?*

* * * * *

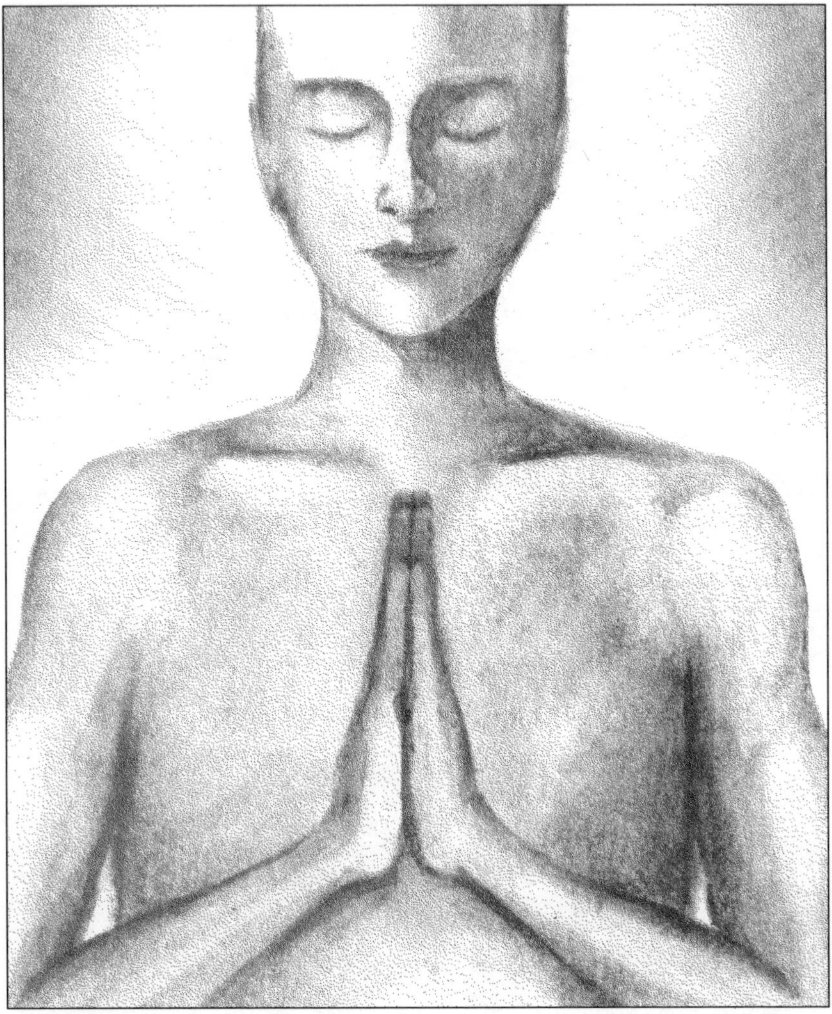

# Lesson Twenty: Prayer

We are the Counsel of Light.

We welcome you to the learning. We are certainly honored to be in the presence of such magnificent beings. It is an incredibly brave thing that you do, incarnating on the Great Mother at this time, to help the world awaken into the age of newness. To have chosen to embark on this journey, at this period in time, for the advancement of yourself and all living beings, is the greatest form of love one can express. It is no wonder that the Counsel of Light is honored by your presence. Peace be your journey as we begin the lesson on prayer.

I am the Voice.

I welcome you to the lesson on prayer. Prayer is a way of communicating with the Beginning Without End. It is also a way of communicating with yourself. It is a way of uncovering the essence of your warriorship. It can help you dissolve the poisons of the soul. It is a wonderful tool given to you by the Beginning Without End to help you go within. Prayer helps the warrior go deep inside herself and examine what her true prayer is. This examination also can show the warrior how she sabotages herself with her prayer.

The Counsel will now take some time to explain the dynamics of prayer and how to best utilize this wonderful tool. The first gift of prayer that one must know is that the Beginning Without End does not need prayer. Prayer is a gift so that the warrior can determine at what pace the Sacred Awakenings will manifest. The Beginning Without End will not give you more than you can handle. You determine at what pace to handle the dissolving of the poisons of the soul.

We shall take a small prayer and examine how this works. Let us suppose the new warrior prays for a closer relationship with the spouse and a closer relationship to the Creator. He asks for money because he needs money. The warrior goes deep within himself and asks to be shown his path and purpose. The warrior asks for guidance from his angels and guides. The warrior knows he has prayed in warm, heartfelt, deep communion with Great Spirit. He knows his prayers shall be answered.

When the warrior asks to be shown his path, the Beginning Without End shall show it to him. He also will be shown what is on the path that is a poison of the soul keeping the young warrior from deepening his relationship to the Beginning Without End. The warrior who looks at this prayer with awareness and self-love knows he is going to have to do some processing of soul poisons before the prayer within him manifests. Because he has prayed and God has answered his prayer right then, the process will start immediately. *You will be handed the process of clearing the obstacles that lie between you and what you want, the soul poisons that block you from having what you want.* The young warrior will learn to use his self-awareness and his guides and angels to help him walk through the poisons, release the love energy that will deepen his relationship to the Beginning Without End, and awaken the true essence of his very own warriorship. This is how Sacred Awakenings unfold.

In this example, the young warrior also prayed for a deepening in his relationship with his spouse. Again, that which is blocking you from having a deeper relationship with your spouse will come up. You will have to go within, find your poison of the soul, and address it, in order to deepen the relationship. This does not mean the spouse has to change for you. This is your prayer and your deepening. Your partner has his or her own prayer that sets the pace of awakening for him or her. It is of the utmost importance that you honor the pace that your partner sets for him- or herself. It does not mean that either warrior needs to speed up or slow down.

You can bet that the largest fear you have will certainly come and visit you. If you, young warrior, are afraid that your spouse will leave you because you deem yourself not worthy, then the feeling that blocks you from having a deeper relationship and accepting the love of your partner will come up. This is not so you can run to the partner and say, "I am afraid you are going to leave me. Please reassure me and console my fear by showing me you love me." It will come up so you can look at the deeper issue within yourself. Maybe your mother or father died when you were young, or maybe you were abandoned (physically or emotionally) when you were a child. Whatever the block is, you must go deeper with it until it is fully present and then look at it for what it truly is. This will then help you unleash the love energy for yourself and your partner. You will see that this wonderful soul has no intention of abandoning you. It is a good idea at this stage to use a healer or facilitator to help you through this. The healer can help you release the block from your energy field.

In this prayer our warrior also asked for money. Since his prayer was "I need money," he will feel the *need* for money. The warrior's true prayer is need. So what will come up are the blocks in him that allow the money to not be there.

You can see that prayer is a great way to help the warrior go within and seek answers. All answers are within. The warrior reading this may have prayed to the Beginning Without End saying, "I want my path and purpose." Ask and you shall receive, dear one. The warrior will first look at what is in her path that blocks her from finding her true purpose. The warrior will look at what poisons need to be dissolved in order to unleash her love energy that creates. This is a wonderful gift, for it allows the warrior to go at the pace she chooses. After learning how to process the poisons of the soul, the warrior can use prayer to help her with anything.

Let us also look at prayer from a very deep place within the warrior. A warrior carries her prayer around with her all the time. It can change and expand as the warrior grows into her Sacred Awakenings. Let us suppose a young warrior has lost her job and her partner. She is hurt and angry, saying, "Why me, God? Life is hard and I always get the short end of the stick." She goes into the bookstore and picks up this book from the Counsel of Light. She learns that she carries her prayer with her and that her prayer is to be hurt, to be angry, and to have a hard life. She is manifesting these beliefs. To transform them, she can go within, dissolve the poison of the soul, and change her prayer to, maybe, "Wow, I'm learning!" Then, "Show me my purpose." Soon the warrior finds self-love, and so on.

One of the most important things a warrior can ask himself is: "What am I praying for and why?" These are clues to self-awakening and transformation. Prayer is the most powerful tool available to the warrior for use in self-transformation. It also is without beginning and without end. Prayer helps open up the essence-self to the love energy that creates. From this place, whatever you wish to create you can pray for, and through you the Beginning Without End will create a life of abundance, unity, purpose, and communion.

What does it mean that the Beginning Without End creates "through you?" You must lovingly go with the Creator through your blocks in order to manifest creation. Let us say that it is your deepest longing to be a musician. You say to the Beginning Without End, your angels, and your guides, "Let us manifest my longing to be a musician." First, all your soul poisonings come up. "I'm not good enough. I can't read music.

I am afraid someone will ridicule me for my music. What if I don't make any money?" The young warrior has to go through the unblocking of these soul poisons to unleash the love energy that creates. Then, the Creator in you and the Beginning Without End (by the way, there is no difference between the two) pick an instrument and go through the process of unleashing the creation of music that is within you both. This is the place of surrendering into the will of the Creator and knowing that your will and the Creator's will are the same will. This is stepping into creation and into your path. The music you will create is not on the Great Mother yet. The Mother is waiting for you to create it to help elevate the souls of the beings on the planet. This will create optimum health, happiness, communion, and abundance for everyone.

This is how powerful a tool prayer is. This need for new creation is sometimes the reason you cannot figure out what it is you are supposed to do. It is because it may not be on the Great Mother yet. Henry Ford's creation was not on the planet before he invented it. This is why getting to your essence is so important. What your purpose and deepest longing is may not be here on the Earth yet, and that is why you haven't been able to figure out what it is that you wish to pursue.

Harriet Tubman was an abolitionist. She had no education, she had no money, she couldn't read, and her body had been beaten. Her job was within her. She just had to awaken it. She used prayer and meditation to help her dissolve her poisons of the soul. This leads us into the next lesson of meditation, dear warrior one. Peace be your journey.

*　　*　　*　　*　　*

*What shall I ask for, oh Great Father?*
*To understand the mind of the Creator.*
*All answers are within.*
*I shall seek the within.*

*　　*　　*　　*　　*

## Lesson Twenty-One:
# Meditation

We are the Counsel of Light.

We welcome you to the learning. We welcome you to the space of communion. It is truly a privilege to be with you while you read the lesson. Now we will learn of meditation. It is a way of quieting the mind to allow the observer within you to arise and help with the great awakening of your soul. Peace be your journey, dear one.

The Counsel wishes to tell you about listening. Listening comes in many forms. There is listening with the heart, listening with the body, and listening with the mind. When the warrior listens with the body and the heart, she is listening from the place of no words. These listening places create pictures in your head. They create feelings in your heart. These places can help you find your path, and they have equal importance to the awakening of your soul. These places within you need to be awakened again, because they have lain dormant since the invention of TV and radio.

In order to create awareness and learn to use other senses, we use the practice of meditation. There are several wonderful styles of meditation and several books written by fabulous teachers on the subject of how to meditate, so we shall not go into how. But we will go into its necessity in helping you connect to your path and purpose. Meditation is also a means to have communion with the other side of the veil. It helps you open up to prayer and quiets the mind so you can hear something other than yourself. It helps create a healthy body by lowering stress. It also helps by creating time to examine your thoughts. It allows you time to check in with yourself and see how you are feeling. Meditation is just being with yourself without judgment. This is a necessary part of helping yourself unleash the love energy within you. It helps shut off the chatter in your mind and awaken your awareness.

Besides helping you with guidance, physical health and awakening, meditation is a form of communion with the Beginning Without End. This is something that is needed every day. This is the warrior's largest task of awakening into the age of newness. Communion is food for the soul and should be thought of as a need because it truly is. It is a need like food, water, and air. Your soul can go into crisis without having communion. The reason TV is so popular is because people try to fill their souls in some way by living vicariously through television. You can escape the pain of your non-communion by watching something that will give you a false sense of feeling great (or by busying yourself constantly). However, when you turn the TV off, you will again fall into the lack of communion.

Seek prayer and meditation together as communion, and feed your soul so you can unleash the love energy within you, warrior one. The age of newness will know communion and will integrate closeness to the Creator with daily living. The Beginning Without End is why you are here, why the planet exists, why you have life, why you are in lesson, and why the Counsel of Light exists. You cannot ignore this any more, for the age of newness is coming whether you join or not. Change will happen whether you want it to or not. It is time for the spiritual revolution. Peace be your journey, dear ones.

*  *  *  *  *

*I am the way, the truth, and the life.*
*I am the way, the truth, and the life.*
*I am the way, the truth, and the life.*
*I am the vine; ye are the branches.*
*He that abideth in me, and I in him,*
*createth much fruit.*

*  *  *  *  *

We are the Counsel of Light.

It is our prayer that you find the Beginning Without End, Great Spirit, God, the Unseen Presence, or whatever you call this energy. For when you do, my dear one, you will have the way of the warriors. You will have found the truth and the ability to create a life abundantly producing much fruit. We bow at your heart and remind you that you are the children of the Creator.

LESSON TWENTY-TWO

# The Energies of the Creator

Hello, dear ones.

We are the Counsel of Light. It is our innermost joy and longing to be here with you now as we bring you these lessons.

* * * * *

*Peace be your journey.*
*Peace be your soul.*
*Peace be your inner calling.*
*Peace be your knowing.*
*We are with you always, always, always!*

* * * * *

It has come time for the last of these lessons. Again, all of the Counsel speaks. Please ask for all your counsel to be with you as you read the lesson.

I am the Voice.

It will come as no surprise to you, dear one, that all has been seen in the here and now, meaning that all exists now. In your dualistic view, you have broken that into time frames: past, present, and future. This dualistic concept of linear time helps the mind grasp the hard-to-understand reality of "no time." We shall attempt to explain the reality to you.

The reality of your life has many, many processes. Some are obvious, and some would be impossible for you to relate to at this point in your understanding. What you must know, my warrior one, is that you have a multidimensional task, and you are a multidimensional being, and what you are physically is not your only reality. It is just the one you give most credence to. Most of your faith and trust comes from your physically-based reality. That is to say, you only believe what you can hear, see, taste, smell, or touch in the physical reality. However, you are more than just a physical being. You are also a spiritual being and an emotional being. These are just a few of the dimensions that you live in. Each of these dimensions has a world of its own. Your natural state of being, within your essence, is in the spiritual realm. This is where you first came from and where you always return when finished with an incarnation. It is your home. Is it any wonder that you struggle and long to connect with home? How can you not become homesick? *While you are on the planet, we miss you, too.*

The presence of the Beginning Without End is the one commonality between all of your multidimensional lives. That single commonality is what bridges you to both sides of the veil. It is what connects everything together and why you can be in all dimensions simultaneously. The work of awakening the soul will be to bridge all sides of the veil until physical and spiritual dimensions are one in the now, in an aware state of being.

The Beginning Without End is an energy, a food, a healing, a being, a Creator, a wise counsel, and anything else you want to include. It is not a dogma, a bible, a religion, a priest, a practice, or a mantra. These are all creations of your world.

To understand the Beginning Without End, you must first look at your belief systems about what you think the Beginning Without End even is. Your planet has many stories regarding that which is without beginning and without end. But if you, warrior one, can look deep enough within yourself, you may find that you truly have no grasp of what the Beginning Without End can be.

If the warrior sees the Beginning Without End as just energy, then what the warrior can learn to do first is use the energy to heal herself. Then she can use it to heal others. Then you may begin to understand how this energy is used. What parts of the energy do you need more or less of?

For example, if we look at the human vessel, we can see that the arms and legs are part of the same body, yet each has a distinct and separate function. Each has its own energy, and yet the arms and legs are part of the whole – a very important part of the whole. Somehow the warrior knows that his body has arms and legs. He uses them and loves them. However, he may not know the experience of arms and legs being there before he was created. Before arms and legs were on your vessel, several vessels before you had arms and legs. The creation of arms and legs happened before you existed. Arms and legs just were.

Now, in the example, replace the vessel with the energy of the Beginning Without End, and the parts of the body with the different energies of the Beginning Without End – the energy of wisdom, the energy of love, the energy of truth, the energy of the Holy Spirit, the energy of male and female, or yin and yang, and the energy of knowing. These metaphorically are the body of the Beginning Without End. All of these energies are without beginning and without end. These are the energies of creation. Each of these energies existed before creation began, and all of these energies were involved in the creation of the Great Mother. All of these energies are within you, dear warrior one. This is what enables you to create.

Deep love of something creates the wisdom and knowing of it. The Holy Spirit sends guidance and direction. The energy of yin and yang, male and female, is what sets the creation into motion. I should be clear that the thing you love the most and is your passion is the largest clue to what your creation is. If you feel something big but cannot find it within yourself, then perhaps it is not yet on the planet, but it has been planted in you, dear warrior one. While you are on the healing journey, you may use all of these energies. They are your birthright and are yours as a gift from the Beginning Without End.

We shall now tell you how to get help accessing these energies. When we go into healing, we can listen to and feel our wound. Most of the time the warrior will know if she needs more of the love energy to help her heal the wound. However, if the warrior wishes to manifest a creation that she feels is part of her purpose, but she feels out of balance, she may say, "Perhaps I need more truth energy or wisdom energy to help manifest this purpose." Then she will ask Creator to send Holy Spirit energy to help the warrior balance energies. This will send the warrior into a space of dissolving her poisons of the soul, creating a clearer path for receiving the needed energy. This is very much what prayer does, warrior one. However, since you have prayer as a tool, you must know prayer existed before the Great Mother did. Prayer existed before all religions. It existed before teacher or priest. In the beginning, there was prayer energy. It is part of asking for Holy Spirit help.

Through your journey of transition and awakening on the planet, it will be most important to know these energies. Wisdom is not something you learn, it is something that already exists on both sides of the veil. Before the creation of humanity, wisdom just was, and still is. The same is true with love, truth, knowing, and all other energies. All of them are yours to use. They will help you awaken to your sacred warriorship, help you have abundance, and help you manifest your sacred purpose.

It is with much dignity that we have imparted this knowledge to you. May it be for the good of all sentient beings. In the name of the Father, the Son, and the Holy Spirit does the warrior walk with the nature of true wisdom, true love, and true light.

Peace be your journey, dear ones. It is no accident that we meet.

** OM MANI PADME OM **

The Counsel of Light

# Resources for Awakening

Unitive Consciousness International offers workshops and training based on this book that catalyse your awakening. To find out more, or to order further copies of this book, please contact us:

**Unitive Consciousness International**
Siddeley House
50 Canbury Park Road
Kingston-upon-Thames
Surrey KT2 6LX
England
Tel: 08700 433 756
Tel: Intl. + 44 ([0]20) 8255 4096
E-mail: mail@unitiveconsciousness.com
Web site: www.unitiveconsciousness.com

The following organizations also offer cutting-edge resources and training.

**Barbara Brennan School of Healing**
500 Spanish River Boulevard, Suite 108
Boca Raton, FL 33431-4559
U.S.A.
Tel: Intl. + 1 (561) 620 8767
Fax: Intl. + 1 (561) 620 9028
E-mail: bbsh.office@barbarabrennan.com
Web site: www.barbarabrennan.com

**The Journey**
P.O. Box 2
Cowbridge CF71 7WN
England
Tel: Intl. + 44 ([0]1656) 890 400
Fax: Intl. + 44 ([0]1656) 890 401
E-mail: thejourney@compuserve.com
Web site: www.brandonbays.com